CHECK YOUR ENGLISH VOCABULARY FOR

LEISURE, TRAVEL AND TOURISM

Second Edition

Rawdon Wyatt

A & C Black • London

First published 1995 by Peter Collin Publishing as
Check Your English Vocabulary for Hotels, Tourism and Catering Management

This second edition published 2005 by
Bloomsbury Publishing Plc

Reprinted 2007 by
A&C Black Publishers Ltd
38 Soho Square, London W1D 3HB

British Library Cataloguing in Publication Data
A catalogue entry for this book is available from the British Library

ISBN-10 0 7136 8736 3
ISBN-13 978 0 7136 8736 1

Text computer typeset by A&C Black
Printed in the UK by Caligraving Ltd

*This book is produced using paper that is made from wood grown in managed, sustainable forests.
It is natural, renewable and recyclable. The logging and manufacturing processes conform
to the environmental regulations of the country of origin.*

Introduction

Who is this book for?

This book has been written for anyone working, or planning to work, in the leisure, travel and tourism industry, and who wants to develop their vocabulary for this line of work. The various exercises throughout the book focus on the key vocabulary that you would expect to understand and use on a day-to-day basis.

How should you use the book?

When you use this book, you should not go through the exercises mechanically. It is better to choose areas that you are unfamiliar with, or areas that you feel are of specific interest or importance to yourself.

The exercises are accompanied by a full answer key at the back of the book. This key also gives you lots of other information that might be useful to you, as well as providing other words (opposites, alternative words, etc) that are not covered in the exercises themselves. There are also some tasks that will give you the opportunity to practise using the vocabulary in context.

It is important to record new words and expressions that you learn. Try to develop your own personal vocabulary 'bank' in a notebook or file. Review the words and expressions on a regular basis so that they become an active part of your vocabulary.

The following books were consulted during the writing of this book, and you might find them useful if you want to find out more about leisure, travel and tourism. The vocabulary covered in this book is not completely exhaustive, so you will also find these sources very helpful if you want to develop your travel vocabulary further:

- *Dictionary of Leisure, Travel and Tourism* (Bloomsbury Publishing, 0-7475-7222-4)
- *Dictionary of Travel, Tourism and Hospitality* (S. Medlik, Butterworth Heinemann, 0-7506-5650-6)
- *Tourism Management* (Stephen J Page, Butterworth Heinemann, 0-7506-5752-9)
- *An Introduction to Tourism* (Leonard J Lickorish and Carson L Jenkins, Elsevier, 0-7506-1956-2)
- *In Search of Hospitality* (Edited by Conrad Lashley and Alison Morrison, Butterworth Heinemann, 0-7506-5431-7)
- *The International Hospitality Industry* (Edited by Bob Brotherton, Butterworth Heinemann, 0-7506-5295-0)
- *Check your Vocabulary series* (various authors, Bloomsbury)

The author also made use of a large range of travel- and tourism-related websites on the Internet, as well as holiday brochures and other information freely available from travel agencies and tour operators.

Contents

International organisations

How many of the international organisations below do you recognise? Complete the crossword on the next page with the words that are missing from these organisations. To help you, the abbreviation of each one appears before its full form.

Across (▶)

4. IYHF = International Youth _____ Federation

6. UNESCO = United Nations Educational, Scientific and _____ Organization

8. EU = European _____

9. ILO = International _____ Organisation

10. FICC = International Federation of _____ and Caravanning

12. ICAO = International Civil _____ Organization

14. IMF = International _____ Fund

17. IATM = International Association of _____ Managers

18. OAS = Organization of _____ States

22. UNEP = United Nations _____ Programme

24. FIYTO = Federation of International _____ Travel Organizations

28. IATA = International Air _____ Association

32. OAU = Organization of African _____

34. BITS = International Bureau of _____ Tourism

35. ISO = International Organisation for _____

36. ASEAN = Association of South-East _____ Nations

37. WLRA = World Leisure and _____ Association

Down (▼)

1. OECD = Organisation for _____ Co-operation and Development

2. CE = Council of _____

3. IHRA = International _____ and Restaurant Association

4. WHO = World _____ Organization

5. WTO = World _____ Organization

7. EFTA = European Free _____ Association

11. WATA = World Association of Travel _____

13. ACI = _____ Council International

15. SPTO = _____ Pacific Tourism Organization

16. WTTC = World _____ and Tourism Council

19. IACVB = International Association of _____ and Visitor Bureaux

20. UFTAA = Universal _____ of Travel Agents Associations

21. IBRD = International Bank for _____ and Development

23. CIS = Commonwealth of _____ States

25. IFTO = International Federation of Tour _____

26. UNDP = United Nations _____ Programme

27. FIA = International _____ Federation

29. ICS = International Chamber of _____

30. ATA = _____ Travel Association

31. WICE = World _____ Council on the Environment

33. PATA = _____ Asia Travel Association

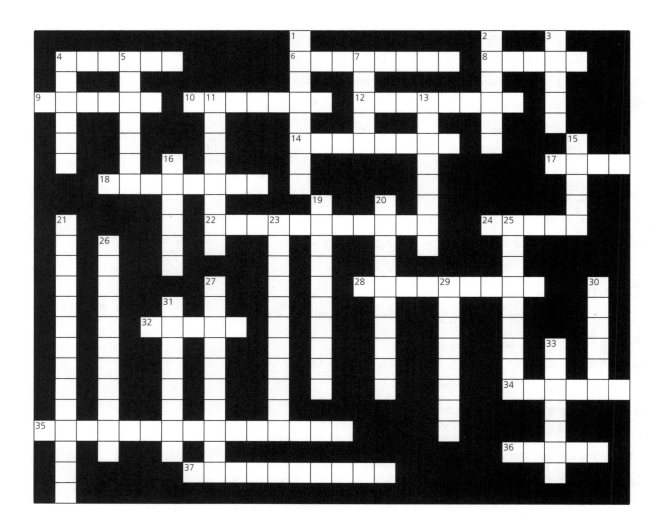

Complete sentences 1 - 35 with appropriate abbreviations from the box. The answer key at the back of the book will tell you what each abbreviation stands for.

APEX	• ASAP	• AST	• ATM	• B & B	• BYO	• CCTV	•	CRS
CSQ	• CST	• DST	• E	• EHO	• ESA	• EST	• ETA	• ETD
FAA	• F & B	• FET	• 4WD	• FFP	• GDS	• GMT	•	HAG
HQ	• IDD	• LRV	• MST	• OW	• PNR	• POS	•	PRO
	PST	• ROI	• RRP	• RT	• RTW	• VIP	• ZIP	

1. A hotel representative will meet you at the airport when you arrive. What's your _____?

2. After several guests complained about poor quality in the restaurant, the hotel hired a new _____ manager.

3. I've checked our computer and I'm afraid there's no _____ for you. Are you sure you have the correct flight details there?

4. The _____ in the USA has banned passengers from taking sharp objects on board aircraft, but mysteriously still allows them to take potentially far more lethal glass bottles on board

5. As part of airport security, _____ cameras are being installed in all the terminals.

6. This is an _____ air ticket, beginning and ending in London, and going via Dubai, Hong Kong, Sydney, San Francisco and New York.

7. In order to improve their quality of service, most tour operators ask their customers to fill in a _____ at the end of their holiday.

8. Passengers who check in late for their flight might be allowed through to the departure gate if they hurry, but most airlines try to discourage these _____ travellers.

9. Some restaurants are attempting to entice customers by offering a _____ option, and charging a small fee for opening the bottle.

10. I'm afraid the flight has been delayed. The new _____ is 21.30, and we hope to begin boarding at 20.45.

11. Passengers who experience long delays at airports are entitled to an _____ from their airline so that they can get something to eat and drink.

12. Most travel agencies have a _____ to assist them in booking flights, hotel rooms, holidays, etc, for their customers.

13. I bought a cheap _____ air ticket to Madrid.

14. We stayed at a lovely _____ last week. The room was large and comfortable, and the breakfast was excellent.

15. For many hotels, their main _____ for accommodation is now the Internet, but many still rely on travel agents to sell their rooms.

16. This ticket says _____. If you want to come back, you need one that says _____.

17. The tour operator isn't very well known. What it needs is a really good _____.

18. The _____ was £75, but I got it for only £25 in the sale.

Abbreviations 2 *(cont.)*

19. It's very urgent: can you contact her _____?

20. First class and Business class passengers get free entry to the _____ suite at the airport.

21. The villa is halfway up a mountain, so you'll need a good _____ vehicle to get there and back.

22. Singapore is 8 hours ahead of _____ , so when it's midday in London, it's 8pm in Singapore.

23. The hotel has _____ telephone facilities, so you don't need to go through the hotel switchboard when you want to make an international phone call.

24. The airline has a _____ which offers several rewards and benefits to passengers who use them on a regular basis.

25. I need to get some cash. Is there an _____ near the hotel?

26. The _____ closed the hotel when he found a rat in the kitchen and two dead pigeons in the water tank.

27. Visitors to the national park are reminded that this is an _____, and they should therefore follow all the rules set out at the entrance.

28. Many Americans prefer going on an _____ when they go abroad, as they feel more secure when someone is there to help them.

29. The advantage of a _____ such as *Galileo International* or *AMADEUS* is that it is very easy for a passenger who is in Japan (for example) to book a flight from Rome to Edinburgh.

30. The airline has decided to move its _____ from Heathrow Airport to Stansted Airport to help reduce overheads.

31. When you book a flight on the Internet, you usually receive a receipt for an _____-ticket via your email.

32. The hotel is at 27 Lombard Street in Boston, but I don't know the _____ code.

33. The hotel chain spent $20m on renovation work, so they are hoping to get a good _____.

34. The American and Canadian time zone on the east side of those countries is known as _____. The other time zones in these countries are _____, _____, _____and (in Canada only) _____ (*also called Provincial Standard Time*).

35. British Summer Time (BST) when the time is one hour ahead of normal time in summer, is known in some other countries (especially the USA) as _____.

4

© A&C Black Publishers Ltd. For reference see *Dictionary of Leisure, Travel and Tourism* (0-7136-8545-X).

Holiday brochure

Look at this (very confusing) extract from a holiday brochure, and decide what the abbreviations in **bold** mean or stand for.

Fort Guadeloupe Resort
Santa Lucia, Camaguey, Cuba

Prices

Prices are all **pp pw** (Under 5's free) and **incl VAT** at 17.5%

SC:	£400
B & B:	£440
HB: :	£470
FB:	£520
AI:	**n/a** at this resort.

Other information

All our **apts** have 2 bedrooms, living room with **TV** and **IDD** telephone, small **k**, large **b** with **wc**, and a **priv** garden or terrace. All rooms have fans and **a/c**. The resort is in an excellent **locn nr** the beach (5 **mins** walk). The airport at Camaguey is an **est** two **hrs** away by bus.

Accommodation is on 3 floors. Please specify **GF**, **1F** or **2F** when booking (although unfortunately we cannot guarantee to provide your choice of room).

Also note that there is a **min** stay period of 7 **nts**.

We must receive **bkgs** at least two weeks before you wish to leave in order to arrange visas. We accept payment by cash, credit or debit card, or **chq**.

All **flts** are with King Air and **dep** twice **wkly** on **Sat** at 8.30 **a.m.** and **Wed** at 4.45 **p.m.**

The resort is closed **Apr** - **Jul**.

Sunlust Travel **PLC** is a **mbr** of **ATOL** and **ABTA**, and is **IATA** bonded and **IIP** accredited. We also support **FOC** to promote a better environment.

We can arrange insurance, foreign currency and **TC** at very reasonable rates.

Accommodation types and tariffs

Complete paragraphs 1 - 12 with the most appropriate word or expression from the box.

> apartment • apartment hotel • boutique hotel • chalet • commercial hotel
> guest house • hotel garni • luxury hotel • motel • tourist hotel
> villa • hostel

1. The _____ we stayed at was right by the beach. It had three bedrooms (all en-suite), a beautiful living / dining room, a huge kitchen, front, back *and* roof gardens and its own swimming pool.

2. The _____ we stayed at when we went skiing in Austria had two double bedrooms, a large living room with open fireplace, a small kitchen and terraces at the front and back with fantastic views over the Alps.

3. It's on the fourth floor. It has two twin rooms, a living room with a Murphy, a small kitchen, a wonderful bathroom with a spa bath, and a small balcony overlooking the swimming pool.

4. David and Buddug Evans are delighted to invite visitors to spend a long weekend in 'Green Briars', the most delightful _____ in Llandudno. Join us for delicious home cooking, traditional comfort and a real Welsh welcome!

5. The 'Ball and Chain' is probably the most exciting and interesting _____ to open in London this year. Not only is it set in the former Chingwall prison, with single, twin and double accommodation in the old cells, but all the fascinating artwork has been done by prisoners in real prisons around the country. Outstanding levels of comfort and service are guaranteed.

6. Driving when tired is one of the most common causes of accidents, so why not break your journey at the Crossways _____. Situated on the A542 between Bunnyhutch and Birdiebath, we offer a choice of comfortable rooms, including three large family rooms, two restaurants and a bar. Ample, secure parking is also provided.

7. For people who want hotel comfort without all the hotel facilities, the _____ is probably the most suitable type of hotel accommodation. No restaurants, no bars, no pools or tennis courts, just simple, comfortable rooms.

8. If you're looking for good, cheap accommodation and don't mind sharing, I'd recommend 'Backpackers' _____ on Wytham View Street. There are three dormitories, each with 12 bunk beds, a café that serves hot drinks and good breakfasts, and the hottest showers in town! The warden is really friendly, too.

9. 'The Moathouse', a _____ outside Derringly, has been designed specifically for businessmen and women visiting the area. Accommodation is in small studio rooms which come with all the necessities for the busy business person. These include complete telephone and Internet facilities, mobile charge points, tea and coffee making facilities and fully soundproofed rooms for a good night's rest.

10. In some cities, long-stay visitors can take advantage of _____. Accommodation is in rooms or

6

suites, each with their own kitchen and bathroom. Normal hotel services are provided, but this type of accommodation generally offers more space and flexibility than a standard hotel.

11.   For visitors with healthy bank accounts, we recommend the Tam'al Dhobi, a _____ on the banks of the river. All rooms are beautifully appointed with king size beds, full bar facilities and stunning views over the river and surrounding desert. Each room even has its own butler, who will take care of your every need.

12.   Holidaymakers on package holidays are usually accommodated in fairly basic (2-star) _____. The advantage of these, of course, is that they are cheap. On the other hand, they are not always comfortable, and can often be in noisy or busy surroundings. They also try to put as many guests as possible into one room: triple rooms with space-saving sofa beds, rollaways and Z-beds are common.

Exercise 2

Look at the descriptions of different accommodation types in exercise 1, and find words which mean:

1.   A double bed which is longer and wider than usual.
2.   A series of hotel rooms (bedroom, living room, etc) with connecting doors.
3.   Two beds, one on top of the other.
4.   A hotel room with two small beds (to accommodate two people).
5.   A hotel room with one small bed (to accommodate one person).
6.   A bed that can be used as a sofa during the day.
7.   A bed that folds into a cupboard or the wall during the day.
8.   A hotel room with one large bed.
9.   A large room with several beds.
10.   A hotel room with its own bathroom attached.
11.   A small room containing a bed that converts to a sofa during the day.
12.   A hotel room with one large bed and two small beds (to accommodate four people).

Exercise 3

The word *tariff* refers to the different rates of costs / charges in hotels and other temporary accommodation.
Match the names of the tariffs in the first box with their description in the second box. In most cases, more than one tariff can be used for each description.

1. all-inclusive • 2. American Plan • 3. Continental Plan • 4. bed and board   5. bed and breakfast • 6. Bermuda Plan • 7. demi-pension • 8. en pension   9. European Plan • 10. full-board • 11. half-board • 12. self catering   13. Modified American Plan

A. You pay for the room only.   B. You pay for the room and breakfast   C. You pay for the room and two meals (breakfast and, usually, dinner)   D. You pay for the room and three meals.   E. You pay for the room, all meals and snacks, and drinks.

7

Airline terminology

How much do you know about airline terminology? Complete the crossword on the next page with the words that are missing from these sentences.

Across (◆)

2. When the passenger wanted to change his flight time and date, the airline had to _____ his ticket so he could fly on the new date.
7. _____ is the practice of refusing to let a passenger check in for a flight, even though he has a confirmed reservation, because the flight is already full.
9. A company which transports passengers or goods is called a _____.
11. A stay for a short time in a place on a long journey is called a _____.
14. An airline's _____ fare is the standard fare that is listed in its tariff.
15. If a passenger's airline ticket has the letters *F* or *P* as its fare code, it indicates that he is travelling _____ class.
17. If a passenger experiences *7 across* as a result of *10 down*, he might be entitled to something called *denied boarding* _____ in the form of money or a travel voucher.
18. Code _____ is an agreement in which two airlines use the same CRS (computer reservation system) identification code (for example, a passenger booked to fly British Airways to Barcelona might actually fly on Iberia Spanish airlines).
20. A passenger who cancels his reservation and asks for his money back will usually have to pay a _____ charge.
21. _____ tickets are paperless tickets that are becoming more common as people book their flights on the Internet.
25. If a ticket is non-_____, it can only be used by the person whose name is on the ticket (it cannot be used by anyone else).
26. When you book a flight, you are given a special passenger number which is entered into the airline's computer system. This number is known as a record _____.
29. Business class is also often known as _____ class.
31. A passenger who changes from one aircraft to another during transit catches a _____ flight.
32. This is a _____ fare, which means that if you want to change your flight time, you will have to pay more money.
33. I took a _____ flight from Paris to Beirut. On the way it landed in Damascus, but we didn't have to change planes.

Down (◆)

1. A stage of a journey. For example, most trips involve an *outbound* and a *return* _____.
3. I didn't have a confirmed reservation for the flight when I got to the airport, so was put on _____ and waited for a seat to become available.
4. When I flew to Melbourne, the flight involved a 12-hour _____ in Tokyo: I had to wait 8 hours for a change of planes.
5. In the USA, economy class is known as _____ class.
6. If a passenger's airline ticket has the letters *C* or *J* as its fare code, it indicates that she is travelling _____ class.
8. A _____-_____ flight is a flight that doesn't land anywhere except the destination airport.
10. _____ is when an airline sells more seats than are available on a particular flight. This happens when they think there might be *23 down* passengers, and may result in *7 across*.
12. On my last flight, I exceeded my 23Kg baggage _____, and had to pay a large amount of excess baggage.
13. Fares are usually lower during off-_____ times, when fewer people are travelling.
16. The airline was advertising flights from London to New York for "from only £50", but _____ at this price was limited to only five places!
19. A non-_____ ticket cannot be used on another airline.

8

21. If a passenger's airline ticket has the letter Y as its fare code, this indicates that he is travelling _____ class.
22. When I flew from London to Amman, I had to change planes in Frankfurt, but I missed my _____ in Frankfurt because my first flight was late.
23. Airlines often overbook their flights because they think there will usually be at least one or two no-_____ passengers who fail to appear or who cancel their flight.
24. Flights to Cape Town are usually over £600, but at the moment the airline is offering a _____ fare of only £350 return.
27. When a certain number of seats on a flight are sold at a special reduced fare, these fares are known as _____-controlled fares.
28. Even though I had a _____ reservation, the airline wouldn't let me check in
30. Your ticket is for a _____ trip. It goes from London to Istanbul, from Istanbul to Ankara and from Ankara to London.

Also see: *At the airport* (page 10) / *In the air* (page 33)

At the airport

Complete each sentence with an appropriate word, and write the words in the grid on the next page. If you do this correctly, you will reveal something in the shaded vertical strip that international passengers have to go through when they arrive in a country. The first and last letters of each word are already in the grid.

1. A passenger who is changing from one aircraft to another at an airport is called a _____ passenger.

2. An airport _____ is a main building at an airport where passengers arrive and depart.

3. _____ is a word which means 'to get off an aircraft'.

4. _____ is the section of an airport where passengers arrive.

5. (*Heard on the information tannoy*) 'Would the last remaining passengers for flight BA631 to Basel please proceed immediately to _____ 14.'

6. All air passengers have to go through a _____ check before they are allowed onto the aircraft. This is to ensure the safety of the aircraft and the other passengers.

7. A *scheduled* flight is a regular flight which is in the airline's timetable, and a _____ flight is one which has been specially arranged for a particular group or purpose.

8. _____ is the name of the international computer system which is used to find lost baggage.

9. Flights within one country are called _____ flights.

10. Airlines have specially set times for taking off from an airport. These are called time _____.

11. Each time an aircraft arrives at an airport, it has to pay a _____ fee.

12. _____ baggage is passenger's baggage which is put into the aircraft's hold after he checks in.

13. (*Heard on the information tannoy*) 'AF flight 100 for Paris is now ready for _____. Would all passengers please proceed to ....'

14. The track, or 'road' on which an aircraft takes off and lands is called the _____.

15. Passengers flying to another country are usually entitled to buy cheap alcohol, cigarettes, etc, from the _____ free shop.

16. The area where an aircraft waits for passengers, is loaded, fuelled, etc, is called the _____.

17. Before an aircraft takes off, it needs permission from air traffic _____.

18. _____ is a word that means 'permission to take off'.

19. To get from the gate onto an aircraft, passengers often use an _____, which connects the aircraft to the terminal building.

20. IAPA = International Airline _____ Association.

21. FAA = _____ Aviation Administration.

22. Baggage which is heavier than the weight allowed as free baggage for a certain category of ticket is called _____ baggage.

23. The moving platform where baggage is placed for passengers to collect when their aircraft has landed is called a _____.

24. The area of a terminal building after the security check and other formalities is known as the _____ of the terminal.

25. IATA = International Air _____ Association.

26. The area where an aircraft waits to get permission to take off is called a _____ bay.

27. When a passengers land at an airport, they go to the baggage _____ area to collect their suitcases, etc.

28. Airport _____ are letters which are given to identify particular airports (for example, *LHR* for London Heathrow, *JFK* for New York John F Kennedy, etc).

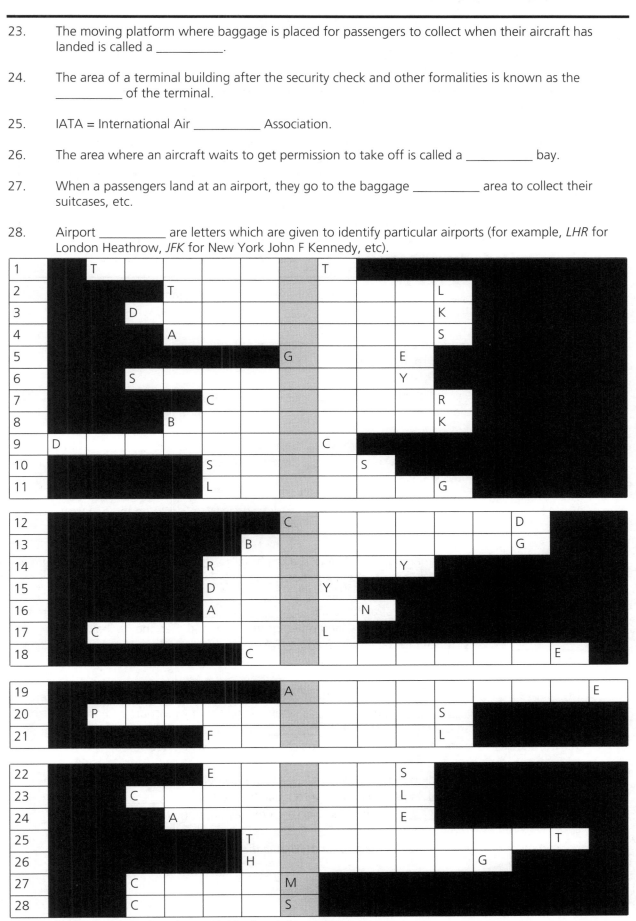

Also see: *Airline terminology* (page 8) / *In the air* (page 33)

At the hotel

Complete the sentences with words or expressions from the box. You do not need to use all the words in the box. In some cases, more than one answer may be possible.

adjoining rooms • airport transfer • ADSL connection • balcony • bar
business centre • cashier • check in • check-in time • check out
check-out time • coffee shop • conference centre • direct-dial telephone
emergency exit • en-suite • exchange / bureau de change • gift shop • gym
heated pool • honeymoon suite • housekeeping • key card • lift / elevator
lobby • minibar • non-residents • no smoking • pay-TV • (swimming) pool
Presidential suite • rack rate • reception • reception room • registration card
reservation • reservations department • residents • restaurant • room service
safe (noun) • safety deposit box • sauna • tariff
tea- and coffee-making facilities • vacancies • wireless connection

1.   Our well-equipped _____ has everything for the busy executive, including a photocopier, full Internet facilities with _____, and _____ to keep you refreshed while you work.

2.   If you would like some food brought to your hotel room, call _____, and if you need new towels or if you want your room cleaned, call _____.

3.   The hotel provides a complimentary _____ for all guests, so you don't have to get a bus or taxi into town when you arrive.

4.   If you arrive at a hotel and ask for a room, you usually have to pay the full _____, but you will probably get a discount if you make a _____ in advance, especially if there are a lot of _____ on the days you want to stay.

5.   Would guests please note that the latest _____ is midday (12 o'clock) on the day they wish to leave.

6.   Guests who have just got married might like to use the hotel's _____, although if they've really got lots of money, they could reserve the magnificent _____.

7.   When you arrive at the hotel, go straight to the _____ to _____. They will ask you to fill in a _____ with your name, address and other information, and then they will give you a _____, which you need to get into your room. Take the _____ if your room is on a high floor.

8.   My room's small, but there's a _____ full of drinks, chocolate and snacks (although I haven't dared to look at the _____!), a _____ where I can keep my passport and other valuables, a _____ so I can call my friends, and a _____ where I can stand outside and get a great view of the city. Oh, and there's _____ so I can watch a movie if I get bored.

9.   The hotel's facilities, including the cocktail _____, the Michelin-starred _____ and the outdoor _____ (which is heated in the winter), can be used by both _____ (guests staying in the hotel) and _____ (people who are not staying in the hotel).

Also see: *Accommodation types and tariffs* (page 6) and *What is their Job (2)?* (page 58)

© A&C Black Publishers Ltd. For reference see *Dictionary of Leisure, Travel and Tourism* (0-7136-8545-X).

Basic foods

Match the letters in column A with those in column B to make the names of basic foods. The first one in the first section has been done as an example.

Group 1: Meat and poultry

(Example: **ba**___ + ___**con** = *bacon*)

A	B
ba___	___mb
be___	___ef
chic___	___**con**
du___	___ose
go___	___ck
ha___	___re
la___	___ken

A	B
mut___	___rk
phea___	___bit
pig___	___al
po___	___son
rab___	___sant
ve___	___eon
veni___	___ton

Group 2: Fish and seafood

A	B
co___	___ring
cr___	___sel
cray___	___dock
had___	___ab
her___	___ster
lob___	___fish
mus___	___d

A	B
oys___	___lop
pla___	___mon
pra___	___ice
scal___	___na
sal___	___ter
tro___	___wn
tu___	___ut

Group 3: Vegetables

A	B
arti___	___gette
aspa___	___flower
aub___	___coli
broc___	___rot
cab___	___ragus
car___	___mber
cauli___	___bage
cour___	___choke
cucu___	___ergine

A	B
let___	___tuce
mar___	___corn
mush___	___on
oni___	___kin
pe___	___per
pep___	___room
pump___	___as
sweet___	___row
tur___	___nip

13

Group 4: Fruits

A	B
apri___	___wi
che___	___berry
goose___	___hee
gra___	___me
ki___	___cot
li___	___go
lyc___	___pe
man___	___rry

A	B
necta___	___rine
pl___	___berry
pe___	___um
pea___	___ch
pap___	___melon
pine___	___apple
straw___	___aya
water___	___ar

Group 5: Herbs and spices

A	B
chi___	___ger
cinn___	___in
cori___	___lic
cum___	___ander
gar___	___lli
gin___	___amon
nut___	___gano
ore___	___meg

A	B
pep___	___me
pap___	___rika
par___	___ron
rose___	___mary
saff___	___per
sa___	___eric
turm___	___ge
thy___	___sley

Group 6: Other basic foods

A	B
be___	___am
bre___	___ans
cer___	___gs
che___	___tils
cre___	___ese
eg___	___ad
len___	___eal

A	B
marg___	___ta
noo___	___hurt
oi___	___dles
oli___	___ce
pas___	___l
ri___	___ves
yog___	___arine

Also see: *Food issues* (page 23)

British and American English

British people and people from North America (the USA and Canada) often use different words to express the same idea. Sentences 1 - 12 below all have words which are specific to British-English in **bold**. Replace them with American-English words, which you will find by reading from left to right (⇨) and from right to left (⇦) in the box below. These words are not in the same order as those in the sentences.

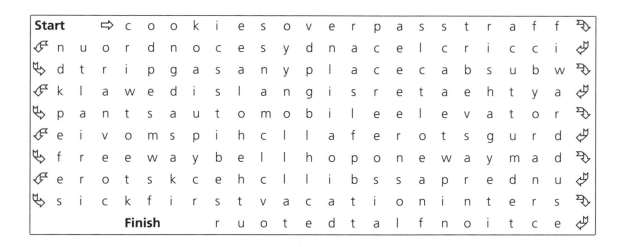

1. The guest in room 314 is really **angry**.

2. The tour group want to go to the **cinema** to see a **film**.

3. The guest told the hotel **porter** to put his suitcase **anywhere**.

4. Could you call me a **taxi**?

5. After eating so many **sweets**, **biscuits** and **crisps**, the children felt **ill**.

6. To get from the **ground** floor to the **first** floor, it's probably quicker to use the stairs than take the **lift**.

7. We really enjoyed our **holiday** in Florida this **autumn**.

8. I looked for a **chemist**, but was only able to find a **shop** selling **trousers**.

9. The customer in the restaurant asked for the **bill**, and paid for his food with a £20 **note**.

10. *Passenger on bus*: "City centre, please". *Driver*: "**Single** (2 words) or **return** (2 words)?"

11. The driver got into his **car**, turned left at the **crossroads**, went straight over at the **roundabout** (2 words), waited a few moments for the traffic **lights** to change, and then went over the **flyover**. Unfortunately, before he got to the **motorway**, he had a **puncture**. After fixing it, he had to take a **diversion**, and then he ran out of **petrol**.

12. Work on the new **underground** station is causing an obstruction on the **pavement**. To avoid it, cross the road using the **subway**.

Currencies

Look at the national currency codes in the left-hand column of the table below, and complete the other columns with the name of the currency and the name of the country or territory it is used in. Choose your answers from the two boxes. The first one has been done for you.

Note that some standard currency names (e.g., *Dollar*, *Dinar*) are usually preceded by the name (or adjective form) of the country they are used in (e.g., *Singapore* *Dollar*, *Jordanian* *Dinar*).

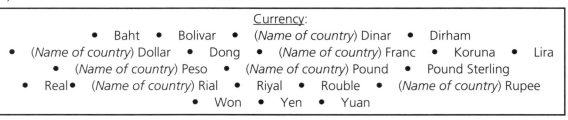

Currency:
- Baht • Bolivar • (*Name of country*) Dinar • Dirham
- (*Name of country*) Dollar • Dong • (*Name of country*) Franc • Koruna • Lira
- (*Name of country*) Peso • (*Name of country*) Pound • Pound Sterling
- Real • (*Name of country*) Rial • Riyal • Rouble • (*Name of country*) Rupee
- Won • Yen • Yuan

Name of country or territory:
- Australia • Brazil • Chile • China • Cyprus • Czech Republic
- Egypt • Hong Kong • India • Iran • Japan • Jordan • Kuwait
- Malta • Russia • Saudi Arabia • Singapore • South Korea • Switzerland
- Thailand • United Kingdom • United Arab Emirates • United States of America
- Venezuela • Vietnam

	Currency code	Name of currency	Name of country / territory
1	SGD	*Singapore Dollar*	*Singapore*
2	THB		
3	KWD		
4	INR		
5	CHF		
6	CNY		
7	GBP		
8	RUR		
9	VND		
10	VEB		
11	HKD		
12	CYP		
13	KRW		
14	USD		
15	CLP		
16	IRR		
17	EGP		
18	JPY		
19	SAR		
20	AUD		
21	AED		
22	BRR		
23	CSZ		
24	JOD		
25	MTL		

Exercise 2

Rearrange the letters in **bold** on the left to make the names of the countries where you would spend the currencies on the right. The first one has been done as an example.

1. **RCDEOUA** = _Ecuador_ (Currency = Dollar)

2. **EARISL** = _____ (Curreny = Shekel)

3. **NOTIEAS** = _____ (Currency = Kroon)

4. **TUOHS ARIAFC** = _____ (Currency = Rand)

5. **IATLNIAHU** = _____ (Currency = Litas)

6. **TVAALI** = _____ (Currency = Lat)

7. **IAENLOSV** = _____ (Currency = Tolar)

8. **IARAOMN** = _____ (Currency = Lei)

9. **KIPANAST** = _____ (Currency = Rupee)

10. **EPUR** = _____ (Currency = Sol)

11. **EHANADSGLB** = _____ (Currency = Taka)

12. **AGINUCRAA** = _____ (Currency = Cordoba)

13. **NEUAKIR** = _____ (Currency = Hryvnia)

14. **IASINONDE** = _____ (Currency = Rupiah)

15. **ALASIMYA** = _____ (Currency = Ringgit)

Exercise 3

Below there is a list of the 12 countries (plus their dependencies and incorporated principalities, etc.) which use the *Euro* (€) as their national currency. You will find these by reading from left to right and from right to left, following the directions of the arrows.

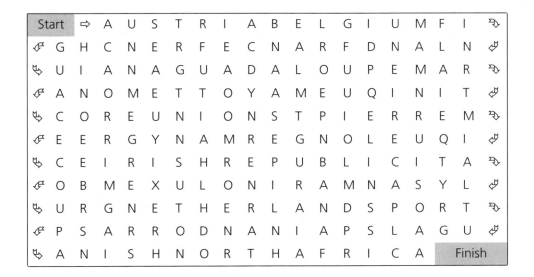

Documents and paperwork

Complete the sentences with words or expressions from the box.

application form • baggage check • boarding pass • certificate of airworthiness
certificate of seaworthiness • claim form • clearance certificate
Customer Satisfaction Questionnaire • docket • driving licence
exit visa • flight coupon • food hygiene certificate • Form E111
health declaration form • hotel voucher • ID card • landing card
multiple-entry visa • passport • Property Irregularity Report • receipt
rental agreement • revalidation sticker • ticket • transit visa
travel insurance • travel voucher • vaccination certificate • work permit

1. Your flight to Tokyo has a 12-hour layover in Moscow. If you want to leave the airport and visit the city, you will need a _____, which you can get from the Russian embassy before you leave.

2. Ladies and gentlemen, we will shortly be arriving in Athens. Non-EU citizens will need to fill in a _____ before going through Immigration, and we will be handing these out now.

3. This is an advance purchase, promotional, round-trip, off-peak, non-endorsable, non-transferable, non-refundable, economy class, maximum stay, open-ended _____. Do you think you can remember that?

4. At the airport, go to the check-in, show them your ticket, give them your baggage and collect your _____, which will show your seat number, boarding time and gate number.

5. At the reception, give the receptionist your _____. This shows that you have booked and paid for your room, and also shows that breakfast is included in the price.

6. When a customer buys a package holiday, the tour operator will often send _____s to the airline, the hotel, etc, to pay for the holiday.

7. European Union residents visiting other European Union countries can get free or reduced-cost medical assistance if they have a _____with them.

8. You should always have _____ when you go on a trip, just in case you lose something valuable, have something stolen or need medical treatment.

9. Some countries will not let foreigners in if their _____ is valid for less than six months. If this applies to you, you will need to fill in an _____ for a new one.

10. There are two parts to your airline ticket: the _____, which the check-in staff keep, and the receipt, which you keep with you.

11. When you hire a car, it is very important to read the _____ very carefully before you sign it. You will also need to show your _____.

12.	In a lot of countries, you need to carry an _____ at all times, so that you can prove who you say you are.

13.	Before you start a job in another country, it is usually essential to obtain a _____.

14.	All aircraft must have a _____ before they are allowed to fly. Similarly, a ship must have a _____ before it is allowed to sail.

15.	Goods that go from one country to another have to be accompanied by a _____ to show that they have been passed by customs.

16.	Some countries may require foreign visitors to have a _____ that shows they are immune to certain diseases that they could catch in that country before they will let them in. Others may ask to see a _____ to show that visitors are in good health and free from contagious diseases.

17.	If an airline loses a passenger's baggage, they will ask him to fill in a _____, describing the item of baggage and its contents. The passenger should give this form, together with his _____ (which shows that his baggage was checked in by the airline) to a member of the ground crew.

18.	In many countries, a restaurant needs to have a _____ to show that it is meets national standards of cleanliness.

19.	Travel companies often ask their guests to fill in a _____ at the end of their holiday so that they can find out if they need to make any changes or improvements to the way they operate.

20.	If you have something stolen while on holiday and want your insurance company to replace it, you will need to fill in a _____ describing what was stolen and how much it was worth.

21.	When you buy something, you should always ask for, and keep, the _____ in case you need to return it.

22.	When the hotel takes a delivery of something, it is important to check the accompanying _____ to make sure that everything the hotel ordered is there.

23.	If an airline passenger decides to change her flight times or another aspect of her flight, it is not always necessary to give her a new ticket. Sometimes a _____ is placed on her original ticket to show that a change has been made.

24.	This is a _____, which means that you can enter and leave the country as many times as you like during a set time period.

25.	Some countries require travellers to have an _____ before they let them leave the country.

Employment

Use the words and expressions in the box to complete the text.

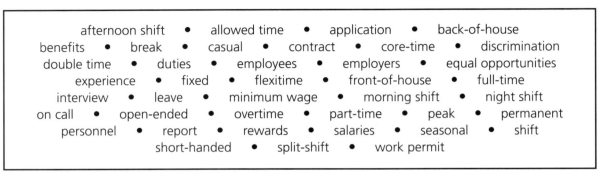

afternoon shift • allowed time • application • back-of-house
benefits • break • casual • contract • core-time • discrimination
double time • duties • employees • employers • equal opportunities
experience • fixed • flexitime • front-of-house • full-time
interview • leave • minimum wage • morning shift • night shift
on call • open-ended • overtime • part-time • peak • permanent
personnel • report • rewards • salaries • seasonal • shift
short-handed • split-shift • work permit

The Four Winds holiday resort in Hibiscus Bay is one of the island's biggest **1.**_____, with an excellent record of treating its **2.**_____ fairly. It pays generous **3.**_____ (which are above the government's set **4.**_____) and offers other **5.**_____ and fringe **6.**_____, such as free meals, free dental and medical care, and paid 7._____ of up to 4 weeks a year. The resort is an **8.**_____ employer, and makes a concerted effort to avoid any kind of **9.**_____. It will employ staff from other countries provided they have a valid **10.**_____ .

The resort has both **11.**_____ staff (those who work all day for five or six days a week) and **12.**_____ staff (those who only work for three or four hours a day, or just two or three days a week). Everyone receives a **13.**_____ which lists his or her **14.**_____ and responsibilities. These are usually **15.**_____ for a period of 3, 6 or 12 months, although some are **16.** _____. The resort also has a number of **17.**_____ workers that it employs from time to time (usually when a specific job needs doing). It likes all its staff to be **18.**_____ twenty four hours a day in case it suddenly needs them. All staff members **19.**_____ to a line manager (for example, head of housekeeping, head of catering, etc), and they in turn answer to the main hotel manager. Most of the work in the resort is **20.**_____ (usually during the **21.**_____ holiday period from May through to October), although it does keep some **22.**_____ staff on the books all year.

For most **23.**_____ staff (waiters, receptionists, bar staff, etc), the resort operates a **24.**_____ system: these are the **25.**_____ from 6 am to 2 pm, the **26.**_____ from 2 pm to 10pm, and the **27.**_____ from 10pm to 6am. **28.**_____ staff (those in the office, for example) can take advantage of the **29.**_____ system, which means that they can start and finish when they like, as long as they work a certain number of hours each week (although there is a **30.**_____ between 11am and 1pm when everybody must be present). Animators and other entertainment staff work on a **31.**_____ system, working from 9am to 1pm, and then again from 6pm to midnight. Everybody has twenty minutes of **32.**_____ for every three hours they work, in addition to a 45-minute lunch **33.**_____ (if their hours coincide with lunch). If anybody is asked to work more than the hours they are contracted to work, they receive **34.**_____ pay (usually time-and-a-half, but they get **35.**_____ if they work on public holidays).

We're a little **36.**_____ at the moment. If you would like a job, fill in this **37.**_____ form and we can arrange for you to have an **38.**_____ with the **39.**_____ manager. Do you have any **40.**_____ in the hospitality trade?

Environmental issues

Fill in the gaps in this essay with appropriate words or expressions from the box.

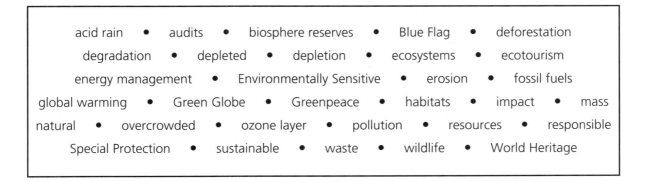

acid rain • audits • biosphere reserves • Blue Flag • deforestation
degradation • depleted • depletion • ecosystems • ecotourism
energy management • Environmentally Sensitive • erosion • fossil fuels
global warming • Green Globe • Greenpeace • habitats • impact • mass
natural • overcrowded • ozone layer • pollution • resources • responsible
Special Protection • sustainable • waste • wildlife • World Heritage

The last thirty years have seen a huge rise in **1.** _____ tourism, and this has inevitably led to environmental **2.** _____ in all areas. Land **3.** _____ such as minerals and fertile soil have been seriously **4.** _____ in order to supply the tourist industry with building materials and food. **5.** _____ of wooded areas and the restructuring of beaches to build resorts have led to soil **6.** _____, while **7.** _____ has suffered as many animals' natural **8.** _____ have been destroyed. Cars, aircraft, hotels, restaurants and resorts, etc, cause **9.** _____ by burning **10.** _____ , and this has led to a **11.** _____ of the **12.** _____ , **13.** _____ , which damages trees and buildings, and a steady rise in **14.** _____ . At the same time, dumped rubbish and other **15.** _____ pollutes soil and water tables, or is burnt to create even more air pollution. What were once areas of **16.** _____ beauty or historical sites are now little more than **17.** _____ rubbish tips, while towns and cities groan under the weight of thousands of visitors.

All over the world, concerted efforts are being made to prevent tourism having a major negative impact on the world's **18.** _____. In many countries, for example, an environmental **19.** _____ assessment has to be carried out before any major tourist development is started, while environmental **20.** _____ are carried out on existing organisations to assess what impact they are having on the environment. UNESCO and The EU are playing a major role. UNESCO has designated some places as **21.** _____ Sites (to protect culturally and naturally important buildings, cities and sites) and **22.** _____ (to protect areas of natural beauty, and to protect wildlife). The EU have designated some areas as **23.** _____ Areas (where they encourage traditional farming methods in order to reduce soil depletion, protect the landscape and protect wild animals), and **24.** _____ Areas, to protect wild birds. The EU has also created the **25.** _____ award, given to beaches which are clean and have tourist facilities which have minimal negative

© A&C Black Publishers Ltd. For reference see *Dictionary of Leisure, Travel and Tourism* (0-7136-8545-X).

Environmental issues *(cont.)*

impact on the environment. Meanwhile, the WTTC runs the **26.** _____ educational programme for travel companies that are concerned about the environment. **27.** _____ programmes are also carried out by many travel companies, which not only benefits the environment but also helps those companies cut down on their running costs.

Is this enough? Environmental support groups such as **28.** _____, *Friends of the Earth* and *Friends of Conservation* do not think so, which is why they will continue to encourage **29.** _____ (and other aspects of **30.** _____ and **31.** _____ tourism), and put pressure on governments and organisations that abuse and damage the environment for the sake of earning tourist dollars.

Exercise 2

Choose the correct word in **bold** to complete these sentences.

1. Paper, glass and aluminium can all be easily **recycled / recharged**.
2. Some local governments **subside / subsidise** public transport so that they can charge their passengers less.
3. Whales, pandas and tigers are all **endangered / dangerous** species.
4. Unless it is checked, mass tourism will seriously **injure / damage** the environment.
5. It is everybody's responsibility to help **protect / defend** the environment.
6. At the **World / Earth** Summit in 1992, several guidelines on environmental action for the 21st century were proposed.
7. The **Tokyo / Kyoto** Agreement of 1997 introduced international laws to reduce greenhouse gases.
8. Many restaurants have responded to the increased demand for **organic / organised** meat and vegetables.
9. Until **genetically / generically** modified food has been proved to be safe, people are reluctant to eat it.
10. Hotels can help to **preserve / conserve** energy by turning down their heating and discouraging the use of air conditioning.

© A&C Black Publishers Ltd. For reference see *Dictionary of Leisure, Travel and Tourism* (0-7136-8545-X).

Complete the paragraphs with appropriate words from the box.

> additives • allergic • allergy • analysis • anaphylactic
> blue • boiling • calories • control • cut down on • diet
> E-numbers • environmental • fat • fibre • free range • frying
> give up • grilling • halal • health • hygiene • intolerance
> intolerant • kosher • medium (or medium-rare) • minerals • moral
> organic • pesticides • rare • raw • religion • roasting
> steaming • vegan • vegetarian • vitamins • well-done

1. Somebody who doesn't eat meat is called a _____. Somebody who doesn't eat any animal products at all is called a _____.

2. Some people refuse to eat meat or other animal products for _____ reasons (they want to remain fit and healthy), some people refuse to eat it for _____ reasons (they believe it is wrong to eat animals) and some people refuse to eat it because of their _____ (belief in God).

3. A lot of people are _____ to certain foods, so cannot eat them. If they have an _____ to foods and accidentally eat them, they will become ill. In very serious cases, they may suffer from _____ shock, which causes shock, breathing difficulties and sometimes death.

4. Some people are _____ to certain foods, so they try to avoid them as their bodies have difficulty processing them. Food _____ is more common in developed countries.

5. Good restaurants and hotels will often send their kitchen staff on an HACCP course to learn how to handle food. The letters HACCP stand for 'health _____ and critical _____ point'. In European Union countries, all restaurant kitchens are required to have a food _____ certificate to show that they can (and do) handle and prepare food safely. If they break the rules, they can be closed down by an _____ health officer who is employed by local councils or the government.

6. The healthiest way of cooking food is by _____ it over hot water, which helps the food retain most of its _____ (valuable metals and other elements) and _____ (naturally occurring substances required by the human body). Other methods of preparing food include _____ in oil, _____ in hot water, _____ in an oven and _____ (also called broiling) under a grill.

7. Food which has been prepared according to Moslem law is called _____ food, and food which has been prepared according to Jewish law is called _____ food.

8.　Meat such as beef and lamb that is cooked so that it is still pink or red inside can be described as _____. If it is still slightly pink (but set) inside, it is described as _____. If there is no pink left inside, we say that it is _____. Some meat and seafood can be served _____ (not cooked at all, such as Italian *carpaccio*, French steak *tartare* and Japanese *sashimi*), and some meats can be served _____ (cooked so that they are brown on the inside, but not cooked at all on the inside).

9.　_____ food (food that has been produced naturally without using chemical fertilisers or _____) is becoming more popular in Britain. People are also eating more _____ meat (from animals which can move around and express natural behaviour). A lot of people try to avoid food that has a lot of _____ (such as monosodium glutamate and other _____).

10.　If you go on a _____, you _____ some foods (you eat less of them) and you _____ other foods (you stop eating them altogether) in order to lose weight. You should try to reduce the number of _____ you consume, and eat foods which are high in _____ and low in _____.

How many other words do you know that are connected with food and cooking?

Exercise 2

The following sentences all talk about food that cannot or should not be eaten. Rearrange the letters in **bold** to make appropriate words and expressions.

1.　When the foods taken from the restaurant kitchen were examined in a laboratory, they were discovered to be **tnotcmdiaaen** with **ribceaat** such as *Bacillus cereus*, *Clostridium botulinum*, *Escherichia coli* and **alamoSllne** spp, all of which can cause **dofo pignosoin**.

2.　Don't serve this bread to anyone: it's well past its **sue-yb etda** of 2 July. It will either be **lates**, or it will have **dumol** growing on it.

3.　The shop was taken for court for selling food that was almost a week past its **lels-yb etad** of 14 November.

4.　Uurgh! This milk tastes really **usro**. It's **nego fof**.

5.　We can't serve this meat in our restaurant. It's **totrne**! There are even maggots in it!

6.　This butter smells **cridan**. Throw it in the bin.

7.　This chicken has been **okdeunrcoed**. It looks all right on the outside, but its still pink on the inside.

Geography

A. Put the words in each group in order according to their size (the smallest first, the largest last). In each list there is one word that does not belong with the others.

1.	city	continent	tributary	county	country
2.	road	peak	footpath	track	lane
3.	mountain	hillock	shore	hill	range
4.	forest	tree	copse	beach	wood
5.	pond	lake	ocean	sea	cape
6.	gorge	plain	waterfall	hollow	valley
7.	gulf	ridge	inlet	bay	cove
8.	cliff	brook	river	estuary	stream

B. Put the words and expressions in the box into their correct category in the table below and on the next page. Some can be included in more than one category.

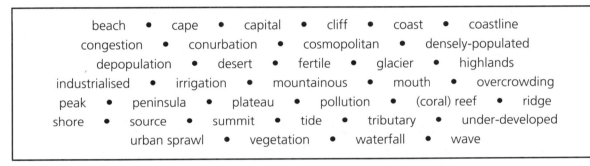

beach • cape • capital • cliff • coast • coastline
congestion • conurbation • cosmopolitan • densely-populated
depopulation • desert • fertile • glacier • highlands
industrialised • irrigation • mountainous • mouth • overcrowding
peak • peninsula • plateau • pollution • (coral) reef • ridge
shore • source • summit • tide • tributary • under-developed
urban sprawl • vegetation • waterfall • wave

Geographical features associated with water and the sea:	Geographical features associated with land, hills and mountains:

Words and expressions associated with agriculture and rural land:	Words and expressions associated with towns and cities:

Geography *(cont.)*

C. Now look at this report of a journey and fill in the gaps with one of the words or expressions from Tasks A and B. In some cases, more than one answer may be possible. You may need to change some of the word forms.

We began our journey in the country's **1.** _____, Trinifuegos, a **2.**_____ conurbation of almost ten million. It is not a pretty place: heavily **3.**_____, with huge factories belching out black fumes, and miles of **4.**_____ as housing estates and shopping centres spread out from the **5.** _____ centre for miles. t was a relief to leave.

As soon as we got into the countryside, things improved considerably. The climate is hot and dry and it is difficult to grow anything, but thanks to **6.**_____, which helps bring water in from the Rio Cauto (the huge river with its **7.**_____ high up in the snow-covered **8.**_____ of the Sierra Maestra **9.**_____), the land is fertile enough to grow the sugar cane on which much of the economy is based. We saw few people, however, as many have moved to the towns and cities to look for more profitable work. It is largely due to this rural **10.**_____ that agriculture in the area is suffering.

Further south, and we enfererd the Holguin **11.**_____, with mountains rising high above us on both sides. The land here drops sharply to the sea and the slow-moving waters of the Rio Cauto give way to **12.**_____ which tumble over cliffs, and small, fast-moving **13.**_____ which are not even wide enough to take a boat. At this point, the road we were travelling along became a **14.**_____, which was only just wide enough for our jeep, and then an unpaved **15.** _____ which almost shook it to pieces.

And then suddenly we turned a corner and the Pacific **16.**_____ was in front of us. Our destination was the town of Santiago de Gibara, built on a **17.**_____ sticking out into the blue waters. The countryside here undulates gently, with low **18.**_____ covered in rich tropical jungle. The open **19.**_____ surrounding the **20.**_____ of the Rio Cauto as it reaches the ocean is rich and **21.**_____, ideal for growing the tobacco plants which need a lot of warm, damp soil.

That night I lay in my cheap hotel, listening to the **22.**_____ gently lapping the sandy **23.**_____, and when I eventually fell asleep, I dreamed of the people who had first inhabited this **24.**_____ almost two thousand years before.

Holiday activities and equipment

Look at the list of holiday activities in the box, then look at the descriptions of equipment, etc, that are needed for some of them. Match each description to one of the activities. There are more activities than there are descriptions.

abseiling •	bungee jumping •	clubbing •	cycling •	eating out
golf •	jeep safari •	scuba diving •	fishing / deep-sea fishing	
go-karting •	hang-gliding •	horse riding •	Inter-railing	
parachuting •	parasailing •	photography •	rock or mountain climbing	
sailing •	sightseeing •	skiing •	snowboarding •	sunbathing
surfing •	swimming •	tennis •	volleyball •	walking / hiking
	water skiing •	windsurfing		

1. A camera, a guidebook, a hat to protect me from the sun, a pair of glasses to protect my eyes from UV rays, and a comfortable pair of shoes.

2. A helmet, a very strong length of elastic, a bridge or a crane, good insurance and lots of courage!

3. The best tackle I can afford (I insist on using the best rods, reels and lines available), plenty of bait, a net and a boat.

4. Definitely a swimming costume, and maybe a pair of goggles, a pair of flippers and a snorkel. Armbands and rubber rings for the children.

5. A swimming costume, a pair of sunglasses, plenty of high-factor suncream, a towel to lie on, a parasol and a pair of sandals or flip flops so that I can walk around from time to time. Oh, and somebody to bring me lots of ice-cold drinks.

6. A wetsuit, a mask, a pair of flippers, gloves, an oxygen tank and a PADI-qualified buddy.

7. A good off-road vehicle or other RV, a map, a walkie-talkie so that I can keep in touch with the other drivers, a valid driving licence and a sense of adventure!

8. A pair of very comfortable walking shoes, a map, a hat or cap, waterproofs in case it rains, a compass so that I know which direction I'm going in, a water bottle and a good picnic.

9. A racquet, some balls, a court (grass or hard), an umpire to settle any arguments and a partner who isn't as good as me!

10. A set of clubs, plenty of balls, a course (of course), a caddy if I can afford one and a partner with roughly the same handicap.

11. A helmet, a good strong rope, gloves or chalk for my hands, boots, crampons, a reliable safety harness, a pick, a firm grip, a good sense of balance and a head for heights.

12.	A lifejacket, waterproofs, a yacht, a strong breeze and some good seasickness pills.

13.	Goggles or sunglasses, two strong poles, plenty of warm clothing (preferably waterproof), boots, a really good piste and a cable-car or chair lift to take me to the top. Have I forgotten anything?

14.	A helmet, some *really* tight, colourful clothes, sunglasses or goggles, a water bottle that be attached to the handlebars, a pump, a puncture repair kit and of course a really good pair of wheels.

15.	A smart dress for me, a jacket and tie for my husband, plenty of money or a credit card, and a big appetite!

16.	Casually smart , comfortable clothes, comfortable shoes (although the fashion these days is to go barefoot), plenty of money for drinks (which are always expensive in places like this) and lots and lots of stamina so that I can keep going until the early hours!

17.	When I travel, I always take my SLR, a tripod, a wide-angle and a telephoto lens, a flashgun, filters and several rolls of fast film. Sometimes I just take my digital point-and-shoot.

Look at the descriptions again, and <u>underline</u> the words and expressions that helped you to decide what the activities were in each one.

<u>Exercise 2</u>
Look at these dictionary definitions. Each one describes a piece of equipment that you need for doing different activities. Each one was mentioned in Exercise 1. Without looking back at the exercise, how many can you name?

1.	Close-fitting glasses worn to protect your eyes.
2.	A solid hat, used as protection.
3.	Light shoes with an open top, made of straps.
4.	Cream you put on your skin to prevent it being sunburnt.
5.	Clothing that is made of material that does not let water through.
6.	Long flat pieces of rubber which you attach to your feet to help you swim faster.
7.	Strong shoes which cover your feet and go above your ankles.
8.	Equipment used for fishing.
9.	An air-filled or cork-filled coat to help you float in water.
10.	A round, air-filled belt that children use to help them float in water (usually used before they can swim)
11.	A portable two-way radio.
12.	Rubber clothes worn by swimmers and divers to keep themselves warm in the water.
13.	Clothing worn on your hands (to protect them from the cold, or to protect them from being hurt)
14.	A drawing which shows a place such as a town or a country, as it is seen from the air.

Also see *Travel items and equipment* on page 47.

Idioms 1

An idiom is an informal expression often used in spoken English. In many cases, the words do not have their literal meaning (for example, to *paint the town red* means to go out and have a good time in the evening).

Complete each idiom in **bold** with an appropriate word from A, B or C. Each idiom is explained in *italics* after each sentence.

1. Despite a huge variety of restaurants selling excellent local dishes, many tourists prefer to eat _____ **food**. (*fast food / convenience food such as hamburgers, pizzas, etc, which are not very healthy for you*)
    A. rubbish   B. junk   C. garbage

2. Airlines are reluctant to admit that delays, poor in-flight service and cramped, uncomfortable seating are the cause of **air** _____. (*anger and aggression often experienced by air travellers and directed towards air crew or fellow passengers*)
    A. rage   B. fury   C. anger

3. The motorway is the quickest way of getting from Paris to Marseilles, but many drivers prefer to take the slower _____ **route**. (*a road that goes through an area of natural beauty, such as mountains, countryside, etc*)
    A. pretty   B. picturesque   C. scenic

4. He's always going on holiday to interesting and exciting places. He's such a **globe-_____**. (*somebody who travels a lot*)
    A. runner   B. hopper   C. trotter

5. Many tourists staying in the area are kept in **tourist** _____ where they rarely get a chance to meet the local people and experience local culture. (*an enclosed resort surrounded by high fences, etc, designed to keep local people out and tourists in*)
    A. ghettoes   B. slums   C. dives

6. Although the flight was fully booked, there were several seats available at the last minute because of **no-_____**. (*people who have booked a seat on an aircraft or in a restaurant, a room in a hotel, etc, and don't arrive*)
    A. appears   B. arrives   C. shows

7. This hotel is dirty and uncomfortable. It's a real _____! (*a dirty, uncomfortable and, usually, cheap hotel*)
    A. doghouse   B. fleapit   C. chicken coop

8. I've got bad _____ **belly**: I shouldn't have had that prawn salad last night. (*stomach ache caused by eating unhygienically-prepared food*)
    A. Birmingham   B. Delhi   C. Bangkok

9. If you miss the last bus, you should take a taxi back to the hotel: don't try to _____ a lift. (*hitch-hike*)
    A. thumb   B. finger   C. hand

10. The resort was **in the middle of** _____, so there was nothing interesting to see or do. (*isolated from any towns, villages, etc*)
    A. everywhere   B. somewhere   C. nowhere

11. Local restaurants are very cheap, so you won't _____ **the bank** by eating out every night. (*spend a lot of money*)
    A. rob   B. bankrupt   C. break

12. I travel a lot on business, so I seem to spend most of my life **living out of a** _____. (*to be away from home a lot*)
    A. bag   B. suitcase   C. rucksack

13. I really enjoyed the cruise, but it took me a few days to find my **sea** _____. (*to adapt to being be on a ship without feeling seasick*)
    A. stomach   B. legs   C. head

14. The barman tried to _____-**change** me: the drink cost £2, I gave him £5 and he only gave me £2 back. (*to cheat someone by not giving him the correct money in change*)
    A. small   B. short   C. little

15. I hadn't been anywhere for years, and then suddenly I got _____ **feet** and decided to do some travelling. (*a desire to travel and see different places*)
    A. itchy   B. scratchy   C. tickly

16. I always try to **travel** _____ when I go on holiday. I usually just take a very small suitcase and nothing else. (*to take very little luggage with you when you travel*)
    A. light   B. gentle   C. easy

17. I don't like staying in busy resorts. I prefer to go somewhere that's **off the** _____ **track**. (*away from popular areas*)
    A. beaten   B. well-walked   C. tramped

18. When I arrive in a foreign city, I can't wait to _____ **the sights**. (*to go sightseeing*)
    A. run   B. play   C. do

19. Passengers flying from Britain to Australia often _____ **the journey** for a day or two in somewhere like Hong Kong or Singapore. (*stop somewhere for a short time during a long journey*)
    A. split   B. crack   C. break

20. One of the biggest problems anyone faces when they travel abroad is **culture** _____. (*confusion or anxiety that travellers experience when visiting a different country*)
    A. surprise   B. shock   C. daze

21. Applying for a visa often involves dealing with a lot of _____ **tape**. (*bureaucracy*)
    A. blue   B. white   C. red

22. £15 for a hamburger and a plate of fries? What a _____-**off**! (*something that costs too much*)
    A. rip   B. tear   C. pull

23. Don't eat in that restaurant. It looks nice from the outside, but it's a real **tourist** _____. (*a place that is in a good location to attract tourists, but is overpriced and generally provides poor service*)
    A. pit   B. trap   C. trick

24. Last year we went on a _____ visit to Europe: we did seven capital cities in seven days! (*a very short visit*)
    A. running   B. flying   C. hurrying

25. The manager insisted our trip to Madrid was for business, but everyone knew it was really a _____. (*a trip that people pretend is for business, but which is really for relaxation and pleasure*)
    A. junket   B. crumpet   C. trumpet

Read the paragraphs below, and match the idioms in **bold** with the definitions on the next page.

A.

You should always **read between the lines** when you look in a holiday brochure. I chose a hotel that was described as being in a quiet location **a stone's throw** from the beach. That was true to a certain extent, but really they were **pulling a fast one**. You see, the hotel was **in the back of beyond**, and it was on a cliff looking down at the beach two hundred feet below! The only place to go in the evening was the hotel bar, and that was a **pick-up joint**.

B.

The brochure told me that the hotel was the best in the area, but to be honest it **fell short of my expectations**. First of all you had to **pay through the nose** for food and service which **wasn't really up to the mark**, and secondly, the manager was a real **misery guts** who complained all the time and kept **laying down the law** ('Don't leave your window open, Don't smoke in your room, Don't make any noise after 10pm, and so on). I met someone who used to stay at the hotel, but he told me it had **gone to the dogs** since a new company had taken it over.

C.

Prices for long-haul flights are usually a bit **steep**. However, competition between airlines has **brought prices down** recently, and if you **shop around** you can usually get a **good deal**, especially if you go to a **bucket shop** or search on the Internet. I managed to get a **cut-price** flight to Perth - £350 return! - but the flight left London at **an unearthly hour** and went **round the houses** (we flew via Dubai, Karachi, Colombo, Kuala Lumpur and Jakarta.) before we reached our destination!

D.

We had a guest staying at our hotel last week. She was a very **tough customer**, always complaining and **picking holes in everything**. Anyway, when she checked out, she demanded a refund, but our manager calmly and politely explained that this was **out of the question**. She **flew off the handle**, told him to **pull his socks up**, and **stormed out** of the hotel without paying! It's bad enough when you get a **skipper**, but when housekeeping went to clean her room, we also discovered she had **nicked** the towels!

E.

I really recommend the restaurant on the corner. You always **get your money's worth**. The **grub** is good and plentiful, and the house **plonk** is **cheap'n'cheerful** (although it might **take the skin off your teeth**). The place is popular with the **natives**, so that's a good sign.

F.

The Aphrodite Hotel in Kyrenia is **out of this world**, and if you stay there you'll know that you're **in good hands**. When I was there, the staff **went out of their way** to make me feel welcome, and the manager **fell over himself** to make sure everything was perfect. He knew I was **dog-tired** when I arrived, so asked all his staff to **keep the noise down**, and of course I **slept like a log**!

1. Get something that is worth the amount of money you paid.	2. Not possible.
3. Very tired.	4. Very good / Excellent.
5. Look for the cheapest prices.	6. A place where men go to try to meet women.
7. Stolen.	8. Slept very well.
9. Did everything possible (two expressions).	10. Safe and well cared for.
11. Local people.	12. Somebody who is always in a bad mood.
13. Declined in quality.	14. A place where you can buy cheap travel tickets.
15. Very near.	16. Food.
17. Very rough tasting.	18. Walked out of a room angrily.
19. Not being completely honest.	20. Somebody who demands the very best quality and service.
21. Made things cheaper.	22. Telling everyone what to do and how to behave.
23. Very early, or during the night.	24. Became very angry.
25. Finding faults all the time.	26. Wasn't good enough.
27. Wasn't as good as I expected.	28. Pay a lot of money.
29. Decide what somebody really means when they say or write something.	30. Be quiet.
31. (Cheap) wine.	32. Make an effort to improve.
33. Very cheap (but not always very good quality) (two expressions).	34. Something which is very cheap and good value.
35. Very remote, a long way from main towns.	36. A very indirect route.
37. A hotel guest who leaves without paying his / her bill.	38. Expensive

Exercise 1

Complete these sentences with one or two words, and write these words in the grid on the next page. If you do this correctly, you will reveal the name of a system that is shared and run by several international airlines (including British Airways, Qantas and Cathay Pacific). The first and last letters of each word or word pair are already in the grid.

1. A captain on an airliner is helped by a co-pilot, who is also known as the _____. (2 words)

2. Aircraft which fly faster than the speed of sound are called supersonic aircraft, and those that fly slower than the speed of sound are called _____ aircraft.

3. The airline equivalent of a *bareboat charter* (see *On the Water* on page 40) is called a _____. (2 words)

4. Aircraft such as the Boeing 737 and 757, which have six seats or fewer across the cabin (in economy class), are called _____ aircraft. (2 words)

5. Aircraft such as the Boeing 747 and 767, which have more than six seats across the cabin, are called _____ aircraft. (2 words)

6. Most modern airliners are powered by jet engines, but smaller airliners are often powered by _____, which are propellers driven by turbine engines.

7. Business class is often called _____ class.

8. The area at the front of an airliner where the pilots sit is called the _____. (2 words).

9. When a lot of airliners are trying to land at an airport, _____ usually occurs. This means that the aircraft fly round in circles while they descend until they get permission to land.

10. A _____ is an aircraft with a large propeller (called *rotor blades*) on top which allows it to lift straight off the ground.

11. On an airliner, passengers can have a window seat, a middle seat or an _____ seat.

12. The _____ are the people who look after passengers on an airline. (2 words)

13. Small airliners (usually with fewer than 20 seats) which fly short routes between cities are often called _____. (2 words)

14. A flight that covers a big distance (for example, Tokyo to San Francisco, London to New York, etc) is called a _____ flight. (2 words)

15. In the USA, economy class is called _____ class.

16. A small jet (usually with fewer than 10 seats, and often used by businesspeople) is called an _____ jet.

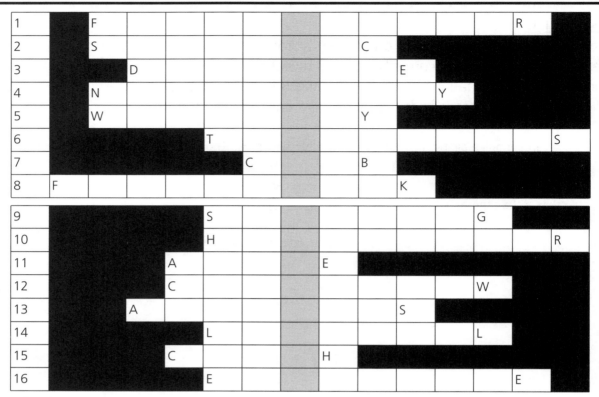

Exercise 2

In the box below there are lots of other words and expressions that airlines use, but they have been joined together. Can you separate them into individual words and expressions? Do this by reading from left to right only.

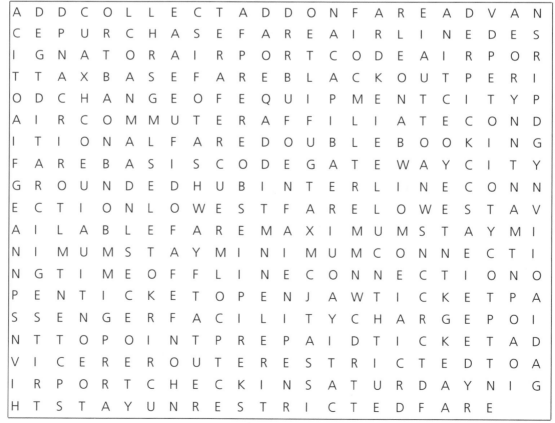

A	D	D	C	O	L	L	E	C	T	A	D	D	O	N	F	A	R	E	A	D	V	A	N
C	E	P	U	R	C	H	A	S	E	F	A	R	E	A	I	R	L	I	N	E	D	E	S
I	G	N	A	T	O	R	A	I	R	P	O	R	T	C	O	D	E	A	I	R	P	O	R
T	T	A	X	B	A	S	E	F	A	R	E	B	L	A	C	K	O	U	T	P	E	R	I
O	D	C	H	A	N	G	E	O	F	E	Q	U	I	P	M	E	N	T	C	I	T	Y	P
A	I	R	C	O	M	M	U	T	E	R	A	F	F	I	L	I	A	T	E	C	O	N	D
I	T	I	O	N	A	L	F	A	R	E	D	O	U	B	L	E	B	O	O	K	I	N	G
F	A	R	E	B	A	S	I	S	C	O	D	E	G	A	T	E	W	A	Y	C	I	T	Y
G	R	O	U	N	D	E	D	H	U	B	I	N	T	E	R	L	I	N	E	C	O	N	N
E	C	T	I	O	N	L	O	W	E	S	T	F	A	R	E	L	O	W	E	S	T	A	V
A	I	L	A	B	L	E	F	A	R	E	M	A	X	I	M	U	M	S	T	A	Y	M	I
N	I	M	U	M	S	T	A	Y	M	I	N	I	M	U	M	C	O	N	N	E	C	T	I
N	G	T	I	M	E	O	F	F	L	I	N	E	C	O	N	N	E	C	T	I	O	N	O
P	E	N	T	I	C	K	E	T	O	P	E	N	J	A	W	T	I	C	K	E	T	P	A
S	S	E	N	G	E	R	F	A	C	I	L	I	T	Y	C	H	A	R	G	E	P	O	I
N	T	T	O	P	O	I	N	T	P	R	E	P	A	I	D	T	I	C	K	E	T	A	D
V	I	C	E	R	E	R	O	U	T	E	R	E	S	T	R	I	C	T	E	D	T	O	A
I	R	P	O	R	T	C	H	E	C	K	I	N	S	A	T	U	R	D	A	Y	N	I	G
H	T	S	T	A	Y	U	N	R	E	S	T	R	I	C	T	E	D	F	A	R	E		

Also see: *Airline terminology* (page 8), *At the airport* (page 10)

Money matters

Exercise 1

Use the words and expressions in the box to complete these paragraphs.

```
advance    •    bureau de change    •    cash    •    commission    •    credit card
credit limit    •    debit card    •    exchange rate    •    hard currency    •    interest
         in the black    •    in the red    •    soft currencies    •    strong
                  transaction    •    traveller's cheques    •    weak
```

When you go travelling, it is always a good idea to take a bit of **1.**_____ (coins and notes) with you: preferably a **2.**_____ like US dollars or British pounds*. A lot of places will refuse to change **3.**_____ from countries with weak economies.

The British pound is **4.**_____ at the moment, so when British travellers go to the USA, their pound will buy more dollars. When it is **5.**_____, they will get fewer dollars for their money.

You can change **6.**_____ at any bank or **7.**_____ in the city, but check the **8.**_____ they are offering you first, and also check how much **9.**_____ you will be charged (this can be as high as £5, or 8% of your total **10.**_____, in some places.

If you are using a cash machine abroad to withdraw money, it is better to use a **11.**_____ (where money is taken directly from your bank account) rather than get an **12.**_____ on a **13.**_____ (such as *American Express*, *Visa* or *Mastercard*) as you don't have to pay **14.**_____ to the card company. This usually only works, however, if your bank account is **15.**_____ and you have sufficient funds. If your account is **16.**_____ (there is no money in your account and / or you owe your bank money), you may not be able to withdraw money from it (unless your bank gives you a good **17.**_____)

(*also called the *pound sterling*)

Exercise 2

Instructions as above.

```
backhander    •    bankrupt    •    bargain    •    compensation    •    discount
good deal    •    group rate    •    haggle    •    kickback    •    overcharged
    overpriced    •    rack rate    •    recommended retail price    •    refund
                single supplement    •    special price
```

British travellers should choose a travel company that is ABTA-bonded. That way, they know that if the company goes **1.**_____ before their holiday, they will get a complete **2.**_____.

If you arrive at a hotel and want to book a room, you will probably have to pay the **3.**_____ (this is the hotel's full price). However, if you book in advance, you might get a **4.**_____ (sometimes as much as 50 or 60%). And if there are several of you, you might get a special **5.**_____ (although this will probably mean you have to share rooms: if you want your own room, you will probably have to pay a **6.**_____.

One of my favourite places to go shopping is the grand bazaar in Istanbul. However, unlike a supermarket or department store, nothing has a **7.**_____: you have to be prepared to **8.**_____ in order to get a **9.**_____, and you shouldn't believe everyone when they say they are giving you a **10.**'_____'! If you are astute, however, it possible to get a real **11.**_____.

The restaurant we went to was terrible: it was **12.**_____, the food was practically inedible and we were **13.**_____ for the drinks. We discovered that our holiday rep only took us there because she got a generous **14.**_____ from the owner (a €5 **15.**_____ for every customer she took!). I'm still trying to get **16.**_____ for the food poisoning I got there, but the tour company refuses to accept responsibility.

Exercise 3

Instructions as above.

backward pricing • commission • cost-plus • duty
fee-based pricing • inclusive • maintenance • penalty
predatory pricing • price cutting • price discrimination • service
surcharge • VAT (Value Added Tax)

When you buy an airline ticket, there are several questions you should ask yourself. First of all, is the price you are being charged **1.**_____? For example, does it include **2.**_____ (in Britain, this will add another 17.5% to the cost of your ticket), an airport **3.**_____ charge, airport **4.**_____ tax or (in the UK) Air Passenger **5.**_____? Also, if you change the date or time of your flight, will you have to pay a financial **6.**_____? You should also be aware that you might be required to pay a **7.**_____ before you fly (for example, to pay for unexpected rises in fuel costs)

Many tour operators, airlines, etc, have a policy of **8.**_____ (they check their competitors' prices before setting their own), and this can result in serious **9.**_____, which is great news for travellers. Sometimes they charge different prices for different groups of people: this policy of **10.**_____ can result in very cheap prices for travellers who are more flexible with dates, times and so on. Some operators have recently been accused of **11.**_____ in order to prevent their competitors from succeeding in the market (or in some cases, to prevent new competitors entering the market). When travel agencies sell holidays or tickets for travel, they either receive a **12.**_____ from the tour operator, or have a **13.**_____ system (usually on a **14.**_____ basis), where they add a percentage to the tour operators' prices (agreed in advance with the tour operator) and charge this to the customer.

Nationalities

What are the nationalities of the people who come from the countries and territories listed below? (For example, *Dr Kali comes from <u>Afghanistan</u>, so he is <u>Afghan</u>*). Set yourself a time limit of 10 minutes and write down as many as you can.

1. Afghanistan	29. Morocco
2. Argentina	30. Myanmar
3. Australia	31. Nepal
4. Belgium	32. The Netherlands
5. Brazil	33. New Zealand
6. Canada	34. Norway
7. Chile	35. Oman
8. China	36. Peru
9. Cuba	37. The Philippines
10. Cyprus	38. Russia
11. Czech Republic	39. Saudi Arabia
12. Denmark	40. Singapore
13. Egypt	41. Slovakia
14. Finland	42. South Korea
15. France	43. Spain
16. Greece	44. Sudan
17. Hong Kong	45. Sweden
18. India	46. Switzerland
19. Iran	47. Syria
20. Iraq	48. Thailand
21. Japan	49. Turkey
22. Jordan	50. Ukraine
23. Kazakhstan	51. United Kingdom
24. Kenya	52. United States of America
25. Kuwait	53. Venezuela
26. Laos	54. Vietnam
27. Libya	55. Yemen
28. Malta	56. Zimbabwe

How many other countries and their nationalities can you name?

On the road / Car hire

Test your knowledge with this quiz.

1. In German it is an *autobahn*, in French it is an *autoroute*, in Italian it is an *autostrada*. What are the British and American words for this kind of road?

2. What is the British expression for a road that you have to pay to use? What is the American equivalent?

3. What is the name of a main road that goes around a town or city (so that drivers on their way to another place do not have to go through the city? Is it:
    (a) a circle road   (b) a through road   (c) a ring road   (d) a round road   (e) a pass road

4. What is the name given to a minor road which runs through beautiful countryside (often advertised as a tourist attraction)? Is it:
    (a) a pretty route   (b) a nature route   (c) a beauty route   (d) an eco-route
    (e) a scenic route

5. Match the British-English words (which are all connected with cars and the road) in the *first* box with their American equivalent in the *second* box:

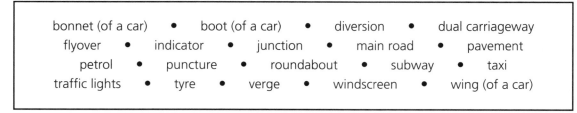

    bonnet (of a car)   •   boot (of a car)   •   diversion   •   dual carriageway
    flyover   •   indicator   •   junction   •   main road   •   pavement
    petrol   •   puncture   •   roundabout   •   subway   •   taxi
    traffic lights   •   tyre   •   verge   •   windscreen   •   wing (of a car)

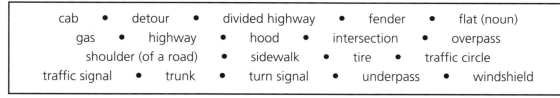

    cab   •   detour   •   divided highway   •   fender   •   flat (noun)
    gas   •   highway   •   hood   •   intersection   •   overpass
    shoulder (of a road)   •   sidewalk   •   tire   •   traffic circle
    traffic signal   •   trunk   •   turn signal   •   underpass   •   windshield

6. Rearrange the letters in bold in this sentence to make words and expressions:
    Drivers in Britain need a driving **eiclecn** to show that they have passed their driving test and are qualified to drive, **enisarcnu** in case they have an accident, and **ador axt** (money paid to the government which allows them to use the road) before they can drive their cars on public roads. If they take their car to another country, they need a **nerge drac** to show that they are insured to drive.

© A&C Black Publishers Ltd. For reference see *Dictionary of Leisure, Travel and Tourism* (0-7136-8545-X).

7.   Match the definitions in the first box with the vehicle being described in the second box.

(A) A car with (usually) four doors which can carry four or five people
(B) A vehicle with an open back for carrying goods.
(C) A two-wheeled cycle, powered by an engine.
(D) A car where the back opens upwards and is used as a door for goods.
(E) A very small car (often for two people) which is very economical to run.
(F) A large car with a flat space behind the seats where parcels or suitcases can be put.
(G) A large car for up to eight people.
(H) A small motorcycle with a curving shield in front of the seat and a platform for the feet.
(I) A fast car, often for just two people.
(J) A vehicle designed to drive over rough ground.
(K) A car with a roof that folds back or can be removed.
(L) A large comfortable bus operated for long-distance travellers.

city car • coach • convertible • estate • 4x4
hatchback • motorcycle • MPV
pick-up truck • saloon • scooter • sports car

8.   Complete this passage about car hire with words from the box.

CDW • classes • conditions • contract
drop-off • LDW • paperwork • personal
refuelling • terms • unlimited

When you hire a car, you can choose from several different (A) _____, or groups, of car (anything from a small group A economy car to a large group 7M people carrier). Before you sign the (B) _____, it is very important to check the (C) _____ (the documents the car hire company gives you) and to make sure you agree to the (D) _____ and (E) _____ of hire. A good car hire company will include the following: (F) _____, which is daily insurance that covers damage to a hire car if you have an accident; (G) _____, which covers the loss, theft or vandalism of the car; (H) _____ accident insurance, which provides life and medical insurance for the driver and passengers; (I) _____ mileage, which means that you can drive as far as you like without paying any more to the car hire company. Note that if you hire the car in one place and return it to another, you may have to pay a (J) _____ charge (this helps the car hire company with the cost of returning the car to its original location). You may also have to pay a (K) _____ service charge to pay for any petrol that you didn't replace to top up the petrol tank to its original level.

On the water

Exercise 1

Match the types of water vessel in the first box with an appropriate definition in the second box.

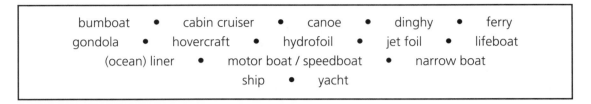

bumboat • cabin cruiser • canoe • dinghy • ferry
gondola • hovercraft • hydrofoil • jet foil • lifeboat
(ocean) liner • motor boat / speedboat • narrow boat
ship • yacht

1.   A boat used to rescue passengers from a sinking ship.

2.   A small boat powered by an engine. These can usually go quite fast.

3.   A small boat for two or three people, with either sails or oars.

4.   A boat which moves quickly over water on thin, retractable legs.

5.   Similar to the boat described above, but with a gas turbine engine to make it go faster.

6.   A sailing boat, or a boat used for pleasure and sport.

7.   A general word for a large boat that carries passengers or cargo across the sea.

8.   A vehicle which moves over water or land on a cushion of air.

9.   A small boat which is moved forward by one or two people using paddles.

10.   A large boat with special areas for people to sleep in.

11.   A large boat that carries people and (often) cars and trucks to and fro across a stretch of water.

12.   A large ship which is used to carry passengers on a cruise.

13.   A long narrow boat with high ends which is moved forward by one person standing at the back (this boat is usually associated with Venice)

14.   A boat that sells food and other provisions to bigger boats.

15.   A long narrow boat used as a holiday home (usually on a canal).

Exercise 2

Decide if these statements are **True** or **False**. If they are false, correct them.

1.   A *provisioned charter* is a system of chartering a ship where the owner provides only the ship, but *not* the crew, fuel or insurance,

2.   Before a ship can carry paying passengers, it must have a *certificate of airworthiness* to show that it

40

complies with safety regulations.

3. A boat's speed is measured in *bows* (for example, *'The ship travels at twelve bows'*).

4. The *stern* is the front of a ship and the *bow* is the back of a ship.

5. The *starboard* is the right-hand side of a ship and the *port* is the left-hand side (when facing forwards).

6. The maximum weight a ship can carry (including crew, passengers, fuel, etc) is called the *gross tonnage*.

7. A ship usually has several floors which are called *companionways*. These are connected by staircases called *bridges*. The *deck* is the top part of the ship where the captain stands.

8. When a large number of boats sail together, usually following one main boat, this is called *flotilla cruising*.

Exercise 3

Rearrange the letters in **bold** to make words. Two words are used twice.

1. A small harbour for boats is called a **ramian**, and consists of individual **hetsbr** where boats can dock.

2. A **nibca** is a room on a boat or ship, and usually contains **hbsert** for passengers to sleep on. An **eiduots acnib** has a window (small round windows on ships are called **htolepsor**).

3. Ferries where vehicles drive on at one end before the trip begins, and then drive off at the other end when the ferry docks are called **lorl-no-orll-fof** ferries.

4. There are several international organisations concerned with sea and water transportation. These include the International **ehaCbmr** of Shipping, the International Shipping **tiadeFnero** and the International **airmeitM** Organisation.

5. **rmbkEa** is a verb which has the same meaning as board or get on (a ship or aircraft). The opposite is **idbrkmsea**.

6. **cesikSsasne** caused by the movement of a ship can be relieved by taking pills.

7. There is an excellent ferry service between the islands, with eight **noscsrsig** a day in the summer.

8. Many ships sail under a flag of **ninvecoecen**, which means that they are registered in another country from that which they operate from (for various reasons, such as tax purposes, more flexible employment regulations, etc).

Positive or negative?

Look at the words and expressions in the boxes below, and decide whether each one has a *positive* connotation (☺: the customer was happy with it) or a *negative* connotation (☹: the customer wasn't happy with it).

My hotel room was:

airy	basic	boiling	bright	charming	claustrophobic
clean	comfortable	comfy	cosy	cramped	damp	dark
dingy	dirty	disgusting	draughty	filthy	freezing	homely
horrible	huge	icy	luxurious	noisy	pokey	pretentious
quiet	roomy	scruffy	seedy	smelly	spacious	spartan
spotless	squalid	sumptuous	tiny	uncomfortable	
well-kept	well-maintained				

The hotel food was:

awful   bland   boring   delicious   different   done to a turn
disgusting   excellent   fatty   filling   greasy   healthy   horrible   inedible
indifferent   lovely   mouth-watering   nondescript   oily   overcooked   overpriced
perfect   revolting   repetitive   rubbery   scrumptious   succulent
sumptuous   tasteless   tasty   unappetising   undercooked   uneatable
unhealthy   vile   wonderful   yucky   yummy

The hotel staff were:

affable   aggressive   amiable   approachable   attentive   considerate
courteous   discourteous   discreet   efficient   genial   helpful   impolite
inattentive   indifferent   inefficient   insolent   kind   knowledgeable   lazy
lovely   off-hand   officious   pleasant   polite   rude   scruffy   slack   smart
surly   unapproachable   unhelpful   unpleasant   warm   welcoming   well-mannered

The tour we went on was:

amazing   boring   dull   educational   fascinating   interesting   intriguing
mind-numbing   monotonous   riveting   stimulating   soul-destroying   stultifying   tedious

The beach was:

beautiful   crowded   dirty   heaving   lovely   overcrowded
picturesque   polluted   rocky   stony   stunning   windswept

Complete these sentences with appropriate prepositions (*in*, *at*, *on*, etc). In some cases, more than one answer may be possible.

1. The bureau de change is open every day _____ 8.30am _____ 6.30pm, but it closes _____ lunchtime _____ Sundays, and _____ the off-peak season it is closed _____ weekends. It is also closed _____ December 25th and January 1st.

2. Most people go _____ bus or taxi _____ the suburbs _____ the city centre, but sometimes it's quicker to go _____ foot.

3. The flight lands _____ Heathrow Airport _____ half past eight, and it should take you about 45 minutes to collect your baggage _____ the carousel and get _____ immigration and customs. If you take the airport express, you should arrive _____ the city centre by ten o'clock.

4. As soon as you've checked _____ your hotel, meet me _____ the lobby and we can go _____ a drink _____ the bar.

5. Your guide, who is an authority _____ Roman architecture, will meet you _____ the ticket office _____ the ampitheatre, and then you'll go _____ the ampitheatre _____ a tour.

6. We stayed _____ a wonderful hotel _____ the sea, and it was only a minute's walk _____ a beautiful beach. I would recommend it _____ anyone!

7. All our steaks are served _____ salad or seasonal vegetables, and come _____ a choice _____ five different sauces.

8. We've just been _____ Italy, where we stayed _____ a really nice Italian family who we've known _____ years (ever _____ we met them in London in 1998).

9. We're not satisfied _____ the service here. Who is responsible _____ dealing with customer complaints, and are they free _____ help us now?

10. If you have a complaint or a problem, please speak _____ the manager. He is usually available _____ the mornings. _____ the evenings or _____ night you can discuss any problems _____ the duty manager.

11. We apologise _____ the delay, and are grateful _____ all our passengers _____ their patience and understanding.

12. The city is famous _____ its beautiful architecture, and it is very rich _____ history and culture. The people who live there are very proud _____ their heritage, and are always friendly and welcoming _____ visitors.

13. Alison works _____ a receptionist in a small hotel (just _____ me). Her manager makes her work _____ a slave (just _____ mine!).

14. We would like to compliment the chef _____ an excellent meal, and thank the waiters and waitresses _____ all their hard work. Between them, they have succeeded _____ making the evening a great success.

15. Tourists often suffer _____ minor stomach upsets when they are _____ holiday. This is usually the result _____ a sudden change of diet, but sometimes it indicates poor standards of hygiene _____ the kitchen.

16. Henry travels all _____ the world _____ business. He's just gone _____ Kuala Lumpur and will be back _____ a few days.

Restaurants and bars

Read this passage, and match the names of the restaurants and bars in bold with the type of establishment they are on the next page.

There are lots of different places where you can eat in my home town. I'd like to tell you about some of them.

Let's start with the High Street, which has the highest concentration of restaurants in town. First of all, at number 7 you will find '**Wok and Roll**', which specialises in food from Beijing and Canton. You can't actually eat your food here, but they put your food in special containers that keep it hot until you get it home. Next door at number 9 is '**Curry in a Hurry**', the best place in town for spicy dishes from south Asia. Opposite, at number 11, is '**Wetback's**', which does excellent *fajitas*, *burritos*, *quesadillas* and *chillis*, and two doors further down is '**Frank's Plaice**', which does lovely crispy battered cod and haddock in the good old traditional British style. There's also '**The Big Munch**' nearby. This place is fine if you are in a hurry and need something quick to eat, but I personally wouldn't touch their burgers, fries and fried chicken without really good insurance: their food hygiene record is really terrible! However, if you like *good* (and safe!) American food, check out '**Souperman**', which is behind the supermarket. There are only six tables, so get there early. Great State-side cooking, and really friendly service.

At the end of the street, there's a new Spanish place, '**Bar Celona**'; as the name suggests, it's a bar rather than a restaurant, but you can get lots of small dishes to eat while you drink. If you want a proper sit-down Spanish meal, try '**Alhambra**' nearby. Their *paella* and *gazpacho* are particularly good. Directly opposite is '**Wasabi-Go!**', which is a great place if you like Japanese-style raw fish; their *nigiri* and *temaki* are the best I've ever tasted! Also on the High Street, you'll find the Westbridge Shopping Centre, and on the first floor you'll find '**Tastes**'. This is the perfect place to eat if you've been shopping in the centre, as there are lots of different outlets selling different kinds of cooked food; you buy what you like and then eat in a central seating area. The food is good and cheap, and there is a huge variety.

Denmark Street is at the end of High Street. There are no restaurants here, but '**The Red Lion**' is a great place for a drink before or after dinner. It's very traditional: no jukebox, no fruit machines and absolutely no big-screen television. Oh, and the beer there is out of this world.

Go to the end of Denmark Street, and you'll get to Mill Street. There are several more places to eat here, starting with '**Mamma Mia's**' at number 4: when it comes to the perfect pizza, the chef in this restaurant knows the importance of having a really good thin and crispy base and fresh toppings. If you like Italian food, you could also try '**Pasta Master**' at number 8. Their speciality is pasta, of course, but they also do wonderful meat, including a veal dish which is, er, *veally* good. Ha ha! For those who prefer French food, you have '**Aux Trois Cloches**' at number 6. This is a small, informal, friendly place with good tasty cooking at very reasonable prices. If you have money to burn, you could try the much more formal '**Le Poisson d'Or**' at number 18 (although be warned, even the starters won't cost you less than £20 each, and the waiters are a bit snobby, especially the sommelier and the Maitre d'. And they won't let you in without a jacket and tie).

Mill Street leads to Venice Square, and there are a few more places here. For a traditional British roast dinner, I would recommend '**Silverthorne's**'. You help yourself to a selection of vegetables and sauces or gravies from a buffet, and then a chef cuts you a portion of beef or lamb. For something equally British but less extravagant, you might like to try '**Rosie Lee's**' for a nice cup of tea and a slice of cake (or you could try their wonderful cream teas). On the other side of the square is '**Jimmy's**', where you can get things like pies, sandwiches and light meals. The best place to eat here, however, is '**The George and Dragon**'. This used to be a terrible place: warm beer, the stink of cigarette smoke, fights on a Saturday night. Then two years ago it was bought by a professional chef and he's turned it round completely. You can still drink here, but there's now also a restaurant section serving superb food. Last month the chef received his first Michelin star!

The station is just behind Venice Square. If you're waiting for a train and you're hungry, you could go to '**Choo-Choo's**', which is in the station itself. However, unless you like stale pork pies, sandwiches that curl at the corners and coffee that tastes like mud, I would avoid this place.

1. Wok and Roll	tapas bar
2. Curry in a Hurry	food court
3. Wetback's	tea room
4. Frank's Plaice	buffet
5. The Big Munch	pizzeria
6. Souperman	Tex-Mex restaurant
7. Bar Celona	Fish and chip shop
8. Alhambra	gastropub
9. Wasabi-Go!	snack bar
10. Tastes	relais
11. The Red Lion	diner
12. Mamma Mia's	sushi bar
13. Pasta Master	fast food restaurant
14. Aux Trois Cloches	Indian restaurant
15. Le Poisson d'Or	bodega
16. Silverthorne's	pub
17. Rosie Lee's	Chinese takeaway
18. Jimmy's	bistro
19. The George and Dragon	carvery
20. Choo choo's	trattoria

Services, amenities and attractions

Complete each sentence with one or two words. These can all be found by reading from left to right in the box at the bottom of the page. You do not need all the words in the box.

1.   I need to get some cash and the banks are closed. Is there a/an _____ near here that will take my card?

2.   To get from Summertown to the city centre, take the number 2 or the number 7. There's a _____ in front of the supermarket. Try to have the correct fare.

3.   The _____, which is at the end of Nathan Road, contains thousands of species of tropical plants, including some very rare orchids.

4.   If you want to get a ferry to one of the islands, you will need to get one from the _____ in Piraeus.

5.   I want to send an email to my friends to let them know I'm well and having a good time. Is there a/an _____ near the hotel?

6.   The hotels are full because of the public holiday, but there's an excellent _____ just outside the city centre which is much cheaper but just as comfortable.

7.   The Blue _____ in Istanbul, with its towering minarets and huge dome, is a wonderful example of Islamic architecture.

8.   The *Fondation Beyeler* in Basel is a/an _____ that contains famous works by Picasso, Miró, Max Ernst and other 20th century artists and sculptors.

9.   Somebody's stolen my wallet. Could you tell me where the _____ is, please?

10. Every Wednesday there's a really good food _____ in the main square where you can buy lots of delicious local delicacies to take home.

11. If guests become ill, the hotel will call a doctor. Alternatively, they can go to his _____, which is just round the corner.

12. I've broken my glasses and I need to find a/an _____ so that I can get them replaced.

C	I	N	E	M	A	A	R	T	G	A	L	L	E	R	Y	P	A	R	K
L	I	B	R	A	R	Y	C	A	S	I	N	O	A	I	R	P	O	R	T
S	H	O	P	P	I	N	G	C	E	N	T	R	E	M	A	R	K	E	T
A	M	U	S	E	M	E	N	T	P	A	R	K	S	T	A	D	I	U	M
Y	O	U	T	H	H	O	S	T	E	L	N	I	G	H	T	C	L	U	B
P	O	L	I	C	E	S	T	A	T	I	O	N	B	U	S	S	T	O	P
S	T	A	T	I	O	N	H	E	A	L	T	H	C	L	U	B	A	T	M
R	E	S	T	A	U	R	A	N	T	P	O	R	T	C	A	S	T	L	E
B	A	N	K	G	U	E	S	T	H	O	U	S	E	Z	O	O	P	U	B
M	U	S	E	U	M	T	O	W	N	H	A	L	L	M	O	S	Q	U	E
T	E	M	P	L	E	S	U	R	G	E	R	Y	T	H	E	A	T	R	E
S	P	O	R	T	S	C	E	N	T	R	E	T	A	X	I	R	A	N	K
P	O	S	T	O	F	F	I	C	E	B	A	R	C	H	E	M	I	S	T
T	R	A	V	E	L	A	G	E	N	C	Y	P	H	O	N	E	B	O	X
I	N	T	E	R	N	E	T	C	A	F	E	O	P	T	I	C	I	A	N
B	O	T	A	N	I	C	G	A	R	D	E	N	I	C	E	R	I	N	K
D	E	N	T	I	S	T	H	O	S	P	I	T	A	L	B	E	A	C	H

Travel equipment

Look at these dictionary definitions, and complete each one with one or two words. These are essential or useful things that people take with them when they go on holiday or visit another country for other purposes.

Write your answers in the grid at the bottom of the page. If you do this correctly, you will reveal a word in the shaded vertical strip which is a general word for things you use to clean yourself (e.g., soap, shampoo, toothpaste, etc).

1.   A _____ is a box with a handle which you carry your clothes in when you are travelling.

2.   A _____ is a small portable electric lamp.

3.   A _____ is a small knife that folds up so that you can carry it in your pocket.

4.   A _____ is a soft bag for carrying clothes, etc, when travelling.

5.   A _____ is a piece of paper or a card which allows you to travel on (for example) a plane, ship or train.

6.   A _____ _____ kit is a box or bag with bandages, dressings and basic medicine used in an emergency.

7.   Travel _____ is an agreement with a company by which you are paid compensation if you have an accident, lose your belongings or have them stolen.

8.   A _____ is an official stamp on your travel documents that allows you to enter a country.

9.   A _____ _____ is an official document that lets you work in another country.

10.   A _____ is an official document allowing you to pass from one country to another.

1.													
2.													
3.													
4.													
5.													
6.													
7.													
8.													
9.													
10.													

© A&C Black Publishers Ltd. For reference see *Dictionary of Leisure, Travel and Tourism* (0-7136-8545-X).

Travel health and safety

Use the words and expressions in the box to complete the sentences.

```
air sickness   •   altitude sickness   •   assembly point   •   carbon monoxide detectors
   contagious   •   deep vein thrombosis (DVT)   •   emergency exits   •   fire alarm
        fire blankets   •   fire doors   •   fire extinguishers   •   first aid kit
     food poisoning   •   health declaration form   •   hygiene   •   immunization
     motion sickness   •   notifiable   •   safety announcement   •   safety card
              smoke detectors   •   upset stomach
```

1. All restaurant kitchens should have a _____ containing bandages and other emergency medical equipment. _____ should also be available to wrap around anyone who is engulfed by fire.

2. Walkers in the Himalayas often experience _____ because they are not used to being so high up.

3. If a guest discovers a fire, he / she should alert other guests and staff in the hotel by setting off the nearest _____ and then evacuating the building.

4. Airlines recommend that air passengers should take light exercise (for example, a walk) during long haul flights to avoid _____ .

5. Passengers on a commercial flight should listen carefully to the _____, read the _____ in the seat pocket in front of them, and make a note of where the _____ are, bearing in mind that the nearest one might be behind them.

6. An ill feeling caused by being in a moving vehicle is called _____ (it is also called _____ when travelling in an aircraft).

7. Hotels should ensure that _____ are kept closed but unlocked at all times.

8. _____ should be installed in corridors and in all rooms, and tested on a weekly basis. Their batteries should be changed every six months. Buildings that use gas heating or have gas boilers should also consider installing _____.

9. *E. coli* and *Salmonella* are just two of the bacteria that can cause very serious _____.

10. In the event of a fire, guests should lease their rooms immediately and go to the _____, which is in the hotel car park.

11. There are two _____ on each floor to use in the event of a fire. One of these contains carbon dioxide and one contains water.

12. Before travelling to some countries, it is necessary to receive _____ against some of the diseases you could catch.

13. Some countries require visitors to provide a _____ to show that they are free from illness and _____ diseases.

14. _____ diseases are dangerous diseases which have to be reported to a health authority when a patient is diagnosed.

15. Many travellers experience an _____ when they visit foreign countries, usually as a result of a change in diet, but sometimes as a result of poor _____ in restaurants.

© A&C Black Publishers Ltd. For reference see *Dictionary of Leisure, Travel and Tourism* (0-7136-8545-X).

Two-word expressions 1: A - Z

Exercise 1

Complete the words in the grid to make two-word expressions connected with Travel and Tourism. You have been given the first letter of each word, and you can find the rest of each word in the box below the grid. The first one has been done as an example.

a_accredited_ agent	b_____ pass	c_____ crew
d_____ tax	e_____ charge	f_____ poisoning
g_____ manager	h_____ charge	i_____ document
j_____ lag	k_____ card	l_____ card
m_____ sickness	n_____-show	o_____ rate
p_____ holiday	q_____ control	r_____ number
s_____ charge	t_____ building	u_____ baggage
v_____ service	w_____ service	y_____ hostel

_ackage	_aiter	_alet	_anding	_andling	_abin	~~_ccredited~~	_ccupancy
_dentity	_eneral	_eparture	_erminal	_ervice	_et	_ey	_naccompanied
_ntrance	_oarding	_o	_ood	_oom	_otion	_outh	_uality

Exercise 2

Complete these sentences with a two-word expression from above.

1. During the flight, our _____ _____ will be serving you a light meal and offering you a selection of drinks from the bar.

2. The best way to avoid _____ _____ when you fly across time zones is to try to stay awake in your new time zone until it gets dark.

3. During the winter months, the _____ _____ in most hotels falls considerably: some are almost empty for most of the season.

4. A _____ _____ includes the price of the flight, transfers, accommodation and local taxes.

5. Some museums have an _____ _____, but others let visitors in for free.

6. Travellers can avoid _____ _____ such as salmonella by only eating in reputable restaurants with a high standard of hygiene and cleanliness, and by making sure that everything is thoroughly cooked.

7. Here's your _____ _____. You're in row 37, seat G. Watch the screens for information and a gate number.

8. Many restaurants add a 10% _____ _____ to their bills, which can increase the cost of a meal significantly.

9. If you need anything cleaning, the hotel offers an excellent _____ _____.

10. The bank will add on a 5% _____ _____ for changing traveller's cheques.

Two-word expressions 2

Choose one word from the first box and one word from the second box to make two-word expressions defined by the sentences. To help you, the *last* letter of one expression is the *first* letter of the next expression. There are some words in the boxes that you do not need.

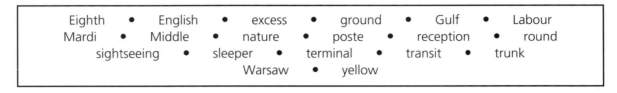

Eighth • English • excess • ground • Gulf • Labour
Mardi • Middle • nature • poste • reception • round
sightseeing • sleeper • terminal • transit • trunk
Warsaw • yellow

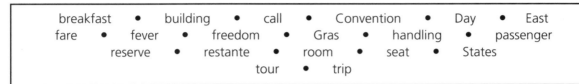

breakfast • building • call • Convention • Day • East
fare • fever • freedom • Gras • handling • passenger
reserve • restante • room • seat • States
tour • trip

1. A world-wide agreement which defines an airline's responsibilities to, and liabilities for, its passengers and their baggage on international flights.

2. A special area where wildlife is protected.

3. A morning meal that typically consists of cereal, bacon, eggs, toast and marmalade.

4. A traveller changing from one aircraft to another at an airport.

5. An American-English expression for a journey from one place to another and back again.

6. A system where letters can be addressed to someone at a post office where they can be collected (called *General Delivery* in American English).

7. Extra money to be paid on trains, planes, etc (such as for travelling first class with a second class ticket, or for travelling further than originally intended).

8. An airline's right to carry passengers between cities in a foreign country (for example, British Airways' right to carry passengers between New York and San Francisco).

9. A festival at the beginning of the period of Lent, and celebrated with carnivals in cities such as New Orleans, Rio de Janeiro and Nice.

10. A small journey (one day or less) which involves visiting the sights of a town or city.

11. A large room in a hotel suitable for big groups of people (for example, for a wedding party).

12. A general geographical name for the area which includes countries situated around the Persian Gulf (but which sometimes also includes Egypt and other countries *not* on the Gulf).

13. The main building at an airport where passengers arrive and depart.

14. The department and staff of an airline who deal with passengers at an airport after their plane has landed

15. A collective name for the countries on the Persian Gulf.

16. A comfortable seat on an aircraft, boat, etc, which can be reclined so that passengers can sleep more easily.

Types of holiday

Look at extracts 1 - 17, which come from different holiday brochures and advertisements, and match each one with the type of holiday it is describing. Choose the holidays from the box below.

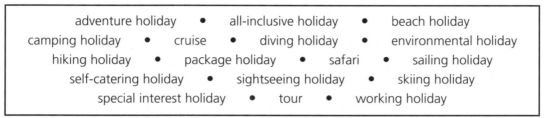

adventure holiday   •   all-inclusive holiday   •   beach holiday
camping holiday   •   cruise   •   diving holiday   •   environmental holiday
hiking holiday   •   package holiday   •   safari   •   sailing holiday
self-catering holiday   •   sightseeing holiday   •   skiing holiday
special interest holiday   •   tour   •   working holiday

1. The Maria Holiday Resort consists of 24 self-contained apartments around a large swimming pool. Each apartment has a well-equipped kitchen where guests can prepare their meals. Alternatively, there are several good restaurants within easy walking distance.

2. What gets your adrenaline pumping? White-water rafting? Bungee jumping? Parachuting? Gliding? Rock climbing? Whatever your choice, Thrash Tours offers it all!

3. White sands, crystal water, waves gently lapping the shore, palm trees swaying in the breeze, a bright sun floating in an azure sky. If this is your idea of paradise, then the Seychelles are for you. So stop dreaming, and book your trip today!

4. The only site in the region to be awarded five stars, the Solero de Risa has pitches for 200 tents, and has its own pool, restaurants, bars and even a small shopping complex. An ideal base for those who like to spend their holiday under canvas.

5. Cabins are luxuriously appointed, and all have a view of the sea. Not that you'll be spending much time in them: with a wide range of activities on deck during the day, and a fabulous entertainment programme at night, you won't want to sleep! And of course with ten cities to explore over three weeks, you'll be out and about the rest of the time.

6. Prices begin from £350 per week, and include return flights from Gatwick or Manchester, visas, taxes, transfers and accommodation. We can even arrange your travel insurance and foreign currency - at very reasonable rates.

7. All our chalets are located within walking distance of the most popular slopes, including the nursery slope. For the more adventurous and experienced, a cable car can get you to the top of the most exciting black-run pistes within half an hour.

8. After a day exploring the area in an open-top jeep, we head for the water-hole at dusk. This is then the focus of all the activity, with hippos, giraffes and elephants competing for space with flamingos and egrets. After that, we return to the lodge for dinner and bed.

9. The walk, which takes in some of the country's most beautiful scenery, takes five days to complete, and we cover an estimated 20 kilometres a day. Accommodation is in youth hostels and guest houses along the way, with breakfast and dinner provided. We strongly recommend that you bring waterproofs and a water bottle, and wear comfortable walking shoes.

10. The Cuatro Vientos resort at Santa Lucia has everything you could possibly want for the perfect holiday. The price of £850 for two weeks includes all flights, taxes, transfers, meals, snacks, locally produced drinks and entertainment.

11. We arrive at Marco Polo airport in the morning and transfer to the city by private water taxi. After checking into our hotel, we meet our guide, who will take us around Saint Mark's Square, the Doge's Palace and the beautiful Basilica di San Marco. We then proceed on foot to the famous Rialto Bridge over the Grand Canal, where you will get the chance....

12. You provide the warm clothes and the enthusiasm, we provide the waterproofs, the lifejackets and, of course, the boats. After a day's training in the safety of peaceful Poliparut harbour, you then head for the open sea for a real taste of life on the ocean wave!

13. The Arrowhead Conservation Centre offers committed greenies the chance to really do their bit for the planet while having fun and getting away from the pressures of daily life. Activities include tree planting, building windbreaks, monitoring pollution levels on the beach and coordinating local recycling programmes. Prices begin from £1200 a week....

14. Day 1: Depart London Gatwick. Arrive at Camaguey. Transfer to Los Pinchos hacienda for one night.
Day 2: After breakfast, coach to Trinidad. Lunch in Trinidad, followed by a walk around the town. Coach to Cienfuegos, staying at the Hotel Jose Martin for two nights.
Day 3: Local bus to botanic gardens for informed tour. Afternoon at leisure, or optional excursion (supplement payable) to Burette lagoon and crocodile farm.

15. Explore some of the most beautiful coral reefs in the world, from the Red Sea to Australia's Great Barrier Reef, which has some of the most exotic underwater flora and fauna in the world. Alternatively, check out some fascinating wrecks dotted around the British Isles. All our instructors are PADI trained and certified...

16. They say that a change is as good as a break. With Hands-On Holidays, you can do both! Grape picking in France or Italy, olive harvesting in Greece and helping to run a bar in Spain are just a few of the temporary, short-term jobs we have on our books. So if you want to have fun and earn a bit of money, contact us today!

17. Take some coconut milk, lemon grass, chillies, garlic, ginger, and fish sauce, mix it together, add some tiger prawns and you've got the perfect Thai meal. Well, almost! Why not find out how to cook real Thai food on one of our residential courses on the beautiful island of Phuket, off Thailand's west coast? Under the tutelage of some of the areas best chefs, we will show you how to dish up the perfect Thai feast!

Look at the descriptions again, and underline the words and expressions that helped you to identify what kind of holiday it was.

Also see: *Types of tourism* (page 53)

Types of tourism

Decide what kinds of tourism are being described, and write the answers in the grid. If you do this correctly, you will reveal another type of tourism in the shaded vertical strip (to help you, the first letter and last letter of each word are already in the grid).

1. Robert's travel company specialises in tourism that tries not to have an adverse effect on the places that its customers visit.
2. The travel company that Olivia works for only provides holidays for people who want to visit other countries, and not stay in their own country.
3. Rebecca's company offers trips to travellers who want to meet and observe indigenous people in their native locations.
4. If you're interested in visiting castles, other old buildings and famous historical sights, the agency that Harry works for would be ideal.
5. Have you been feeling under the weather recently? Whether you want a month in a spa, or just a few days breathing clean mountain air, Harriet's tour company will get you back in the pink again!
6. Fed up with the beach? Can't face another skiing holiday? Well, what about a week on a farm instead? Andy's Tours has a wide range of cottages, caravans and other accommodation in some of the country's most beautiful locations.
7. Bert's tour operator provides transport, accommodation and other travel services for some of the biggest companies in the country.
8. Hilda's Holidays has some of the loudest, liveliest and most exciting resorts available. Why spend a fortnight sitting on a beach when you can spend it drinking yourself under the table?!
9. Ian's company provides accommodation, transport and tours for visitors coming from outside the country.
10. If you want to visit some of the world's most important holy places, Rachel's company is the one to have faith in.
11. Many companies like to reward their employees for working hard and getting good results. Some of them use Imogen's tour operator to book holidays and trips for their best staff to say 'Thank you for all your good work'.

1.	■	■	R		▒									E
2.	■	■		O	▒						D	■	■	■
3.	R				S▒	■	■	■	■	■	■	■	■	■
4.	H				▒			E	■	■	■	■	■	■
5.	■		H		▒			H	■	■	■	■	■	■
6.	■	A			▒									L
7.	B				▒			S	■	■	■	■	■	■
8.	■	■		H	▒		D	■	■	■	■	■	■	■
9.	■		I		▒				D	■	■	■	■	■
10.	■		R		▒						S	■	■	■
11.	■		I		▒					E	■	■	■	■

Also see: *Types of holiday* (page 51)

What has gone wrong?

Look at the situations and what the people are saying on the next two pages, and decide what has happened in each case. Complete each situation with an appropriate word from the first box. You do not need all of the words in the box.

broken • bumped • burnt • cancelled • damaged
delayed • diverted • double-booked • killed • lost
misinformed • mugged • opened • overcharged • overcooked
poisoned • re-routed • robbed • run over / knocked down (by a car)
short-changed • stolen • undercharged • undercooked

Situation 1: A customer in a restaurant is talking to a waiter:
"I asked for it to be well-done, but this is rare. In fact, it's almost raw!"
His food has been _____.

Situation 2: The same customer is talking to the waiter again:
"I think there's a mistake on my bill. I didn't order half of these things".
He has been _____.

Situation 3: An airline passenger is at the airport:
"We were supposed to take off an hour ago. I keep checking the boards for information, but all it says is 'Wait in lounge'."
Her flight has been _____.

Situation 4: An airline passenger is talking to a member of the airline's ground-crew staff:
"Look, I've got two baggage checks, so where's my second item? I've been waiting here for half an hour and it hasn't come through on the luggage carousel."
Some of his luggage has been _____.

Situation 5: A tourist is talking to a police officer:
"I was walking back to my hotel when someone hit me on the head and stole my wallet"
The tourist has been _____ .

Situation 6: A hotel receptionist is talking to a customer.
"I'm sorry, madam, I don't know how it happened, but it looks like the room you reserved has been given to someone else".
The customer's room has been _____.

Situation 7: A train passenger is complaining to a member of railway staff.
"Your ticket booking office told me that the train leaves at nine o'clock every morning, but when I got to the station, I discovered it leaves at half past eight".
The passenger has been _____.

© A&C Black Publishers Ltd. For reference see *Dictionary of Leisure, Travel and Tourism* (0-7136-8545-X).

Situation 8: An airline passenger is calling her family from an aircraft phone.
"*We can't land at O'Hare because of the snow, so they're flying us on to Des Moines and then putting us on a bus*".
The passenger's flight has been _____ because of bad weather.

Situation 9: A passenger in a taxi is complaining to the driver.
"*According to your meter, the fare from the airport is €18. I gave you a €50 note, and you've only given me €20 back.*"
The taxi driver has _____ his passenger.

Situation 10: A woman is at the doctor.
"*I'm getting continual stomach cramps, I've got awful diarrhoea and I can't stop vomiting. It must have been the shellfish I had for dinner last night. I thought it tasted strange*"
The woman has been _____ by eating bad seafood.

Situation 11: A customer in a bar is talking to the barman.
"*I only put the mobile down on the table for a few moments, and when I next looked it had gone. Are you sure you didn't see anything?*"
The customer's mobile phone has (probably) been _____.

Situation 12: A man is at the chemist.
"*I didn't realise how strong the sun was. I fell asleep, and when I woke up I was red and sore from head to toe. Can you give me something to help it?*"
He has been _____ by the sun.

Situation 13: A hotel guest is talking to the hotel manager.
"*When I got back to my room, I discovered that my safe had been broken into, and my passport and money stolen*".
The guest's hotel room has been _____.

Situation 14: A hotel guest is complaining to the hotel's laundry manager.
"*This suit was in perfect condition when I gave it to you to be washed. Now there are three buttons missing and a large tear in one of the jacket sleeves*".
The guest's suit has been _____.

Situation 15: An airline passenger is talking to the check-in assistant.
"*I have a valid ticket for this flight, and I'm in plenty of time to check in, so why are you telling me there are no seats available?*"
The passenger has been _____ by the airline.

© A&C Black Publishers Ltd. For reference see *Dictionary of Leisure, Travel and Tourism* (0-7136-8545-X).

What is their job 1?

Read these descriptions given by people working in jobs related to the travel, tourism and entertainment industry. Can you work out what their jobs are from some of the key words and phrases they use?

1. People call us trolley dollies, but we do much more than just feed people and give them drinks. For a start, we need to make sure that everyone has fastened their safety belt and that their seats are in the upright position before we take-off. We are responsible for demonstrating the safety procedures, and for making sure that people obey the rules during the flight. If there's an accident, we need to make sure that everyone gets out.

2. It's not so bad with small groups, but with big groups it can get really confusing, especially if the place we're visiting is very busy. People might accidentally join another group, or wander off to take a photograph and then get lost, and I spend all my time running around looking for them, waving my umbrella in the air. Most people are attentive and well-behaved, but some don't listen and then ask really stupid questions, or interrupt you to say 'But my guidebook says......'.

3. It's usually quiet until the second sitting at 8 o'clock, then things get really busy. On some nights, there can be as many as 50 covers. There's always so much to remember: who ordered what, whether they wanted still or sparkling water, whether they wanted the meat done rare or medium, was it the house red or the Pinot Noir they wanted, who had the allergy to nuts, who couldn't eat cheese, and so on. And then there are the complainers to deal with. For them, things are always too hot, too cold, overcooked, undercooked, arrived too late, too early or not at all, etc.

4. After receiving our briefing and route, we meet the cabin crew. The first officer and I do a 360 degree outside check, then board and run another complete check on the flight deck. We wait for instructions from the tower, and as soon as we have our slot, we push-back from the terminal building. We taxi across the apron towards the runway and join the queue of others waiting for clearance to take off. Minutes later, we're off the ground and on our way.

5. The job is very routine. We cross-check people's tickets with the information on the computer, then look at their passports to make sure they are who they say they are. We ask them how many items of baggage they have (we need to know what is going in the hold and what they are taking on as hand baggage), whether they packed them themselves, whether they are carrying any sharp or illegal objects in their hand baggage, and whether anyone could have interfered with their bags. We then ask them if they have a seat preference - window or aisle - give them their boarding cards and tell them which gate to go to.

6. Most people want a simple package tour, and come to us for a brochure. Of course, we do a lot more than just hand out brochures. We book holidays, look for the cheapest flights, check accommodation availability, confirm bookings, sell traveller's cheques, foreign currency and insurance, make recommendations and suggestions and generally answer people's travel enquiries. We also have several corporate clients who use us for their business trips. We're a member of ABTA, and have ATOL, by the way, so you know you're in good hands.

7. My duties include meeting our customers at the airport and making them feel welcome, accompanying them to their accommodation and giving them some basic information to familiarise them with their surroundings. The next day, I meet them to tell them about the area, and also to tell them about some of the things they can do and places they can visit. I try to sell them tours, but a lot of people (especially the more independent travellers) tend to make their own arrangements. I also deal with customers' problems as they arise.

8.		I really enjoy my job. I'm quite a sociable person, so it gives me the chance to meet a lot of people. Of course, when things get really busy, I just say 'What can I get you?' or 'Would you like ice and lemon with that?', so the conversation isn't always so great. Sometimes, people have a bit too much and get drunk, which is OK unless they get aggressive too, and start fights. I'm on my feet most of the time, so after a hard night's work I can be absolutely exhausted. Oh, and the money is terrible, but I sometimes get good tips from the customers.

9.		I don't usually talk to the fares I pick up at the rank, but occasionally I get a friendly or talkative customer. Mind you, it can be a bit distracting if I'm trying to concentrate on the road, especially during rush hour, and there's someone in the back seat chatting away. I don't really mind, though, especially if they give me a good tip.

10.		For some people, I'm an essential part of their entertainment experience, to others I'm just a noise (sometimes a rather irritating noise!) in the background. But I like to think that most people enjoy having a nice tune going on in the background, something they can hum or even sing along to while they sip their cocktail. I get requests, as well, so my repertoire of 500 songs can really come in handy. I don't sing along, though, as I have a terrible singing voice. In fact, I'm almost completely tone deaf!

11.		My beat is usually from eight a.m. to 4 p.m. . I spend most of my time on my feet, so at the end of the day I'm quite exhausted. My duties are quite varied, and range from keeping an eye out for pickpockets, ticket touts, dishonest taxi drivers and other rip-off merchants to dealing with tourists who have been victims of crime, and occasionally dealing with a case of shoplifting. The most important thing is to remain highly visible at all times (the uniform helps, of course), so that the bad guys keep away and the tourists can see I'm there to help them if they have problems.

12.		A lot of people are happy to spend their days lounging by the pool, but quite a few actually want to do something, so that's where I come in. A typical day goes like this: at nine, I do a session of pool aerobics, then at ten there's beach volleyball, followed by face painting for the children. After lunch, I give a cooking demonstration and this is followed by some silly games on the beach, which are great fun for adults and children. In the late afternoon, I take the guests on a walk to a nearby village, where we all have a drink. In the evening, there's usually karaoke, a casino night or a disco to organise.

13.		After collecting their things from the carousel, most people go through the green channel: very few go through the red channel, even if they're over the limit on their duty free allowance. It's my job to stop anyone who's trying to get through without paying the relevant import duty. It's also my job to make sure that people don't bring anything illegal into the country. This includes drugs, firearms and explosives. You would be amazed at the things people do to try to smuggle things into the country; last week we stopped someone with twenty gold watches hidden in an artificial leg!

Look at the descriptions again, and underline the key words and expressions that helped you to identify the jobs.

What is their job 2?: Hotel staff

Read this description of a hotel, and match the names of the people in **bold** with their jobs on the next page.

Hello, and welcome to Eynsham Towers International Hotel. My name's **Lisa Apps**, and I'm responsible for the successful running of the hotel. Let me take you round and introduce you to the rest of the staff.

Let's begin at the front. The man standing by the entrance in the uniform and funny hat is **Richard Taylor**. When guests arrive, he's usually the first person they meet. He'll open your taxi door for you, then welcome you into the hotel. The young man standing next to him is **Geoff Walton**, who will carry your bags in and up to your room. The other young man with them is **Mark Adamson**. If you arrive in your own vehicle, he'll take your keys and park up for you. To tell you the truth, he's a terrible driver: I certainly wouldn't trust him with *my* Ferrari!

All right, let's go inside. The man behind the desk by the door is **Brian Richards**. If you want to book a taxi, get tickets for a show, hire a tour guide or anything like that, you should talk to him. The woman behind the desk at the back of the foyer is **Jane Byrne**. She's the person who checks guests in, gives them their keys, takes messages for them, and so on. Next to her is **Jack Grant**. He's the person that guests pay when they leave, and he'll also change traveller's cheques or get you cash on your credit or debit card. The woman behind the desk to your right is **Imogen Bradley**: if guests want to book an air or train ticket, make a reservation at another hotel somewhere else or even book a full package holiday, they can speak to her.

Let's go through this door. We're now in housekeeping, and this is **Emma Ranscombe**, one of the people who cleans the rooms, makes the beds, provides guests with sheets, clean towels, toiletries and so on. The next door takes us through to the administration office, where I work. The young lady sitting at that desk deals with all my correspondence and helps me out with general duties; her name's **Felicity Mills**. Over there by the window is **Jennifer Bryant**. Our hotel has facilities for business meetings and so on, and it's her job to organise these for the companies who use this facility. The man at the other desk is **Robin Buxton**, who is in charge of the hotel finances. Hi, Robin. Is that a new Rolex you're wearing? Very nice.

OK, let's go into the restaurant. It's really busy at the moment because we've just started lunch. This is the person who is responsible for the successful running of the restaurant: **Roger Samson**. Good morning, Roger. The two people over there are **Maria Wade** and **Peter Mann**, who take customers orders and serve their food. The man standing by the bar with the big red nose is **Martin Blackwell**. He's our resident wine expert, and he will help you to choose the perfect bottle of wine to go with your meal. And this young lady is **Kitty Hannah**. She meets customers when they come in and takes them to their table. She also adds up the customers' bills. Hello, Kitty.

Finally, let's go through to the kitchen. It's hot and noisy, isn't it? Right, well, the woman stirring that big pot is **Hilary Eccleston**, and she's one of the people who assists the man over there shouting at everyone. His name's **Gordon Rhodes-Thomson**, and he is in charge of the kitchen. Good morning, Gordon, how are things going? I beg your pardon? Well, really! The same to you. Finally, the young man washing the plates and glasses is **Laurence Bailey**. Uh, Laurence, that glass you just dropped is coming out of your wages, lad.

1. Lisa Apps	meetings and conventions planner
2. Richard Taylor	chambermaid
3. Geoff Walton	concierge
4. Mark Adamson	head chef
5. Brian Richards	waiter
6. Jane Byrne	cashier
7. Jack Grant	commissionaire
8. Imogen Bradley	sommelier
9. Emma Ranscombe	porter
10. Felicity Mills	waitress
11. Jennifer Bryant	manager
12. Robin Buxton	plongeur
13. Roger Samson	sous chef
14. Maria Wade	travel agent
15. Peter Mann	Maitre d'hôtel
16. Martin Blackwell	comptroller
17. Kitty Hannah	valet
18. Hilary Eccleston	greeter
19. Gordon Rhodes-Thomson	personal assistant
20. Laurence Bailey	receptionist

Where are they (1)?

Look at these extracts from conversations, notices, etc, and decide where you would hear or read each one. Choose from the list in the box. Underline the key words that help you decide your answer. Answers may be used more than once.

> At the airport   •   At a ferry terminal   •   On a bus   •   On a cruise ship
> On a safari   •   On a sightseeing tour   •   On the beach   •   On an aircraft
> In a pub or bar   •   In a hotel   •   In a museum   •   In a restaurant
> In a taxi   •   In a theatre   •   In an Internet café

---

1. (On the phone)
    Speaker 1: I'd like to order some food, please.
    Speaker 2: Certainly, madam. I'll put you through to room service.
    Speaker 1: Oh, and I don't seem to have any towels.
    Speaker 2: I'll get housekeeping to send some up. Room 501, isn't it?

2. (Notice) This is a residential district. In the interest of our neighbours, customers are politely requested to keep noise to a minimum when leaving this establishment.

3. All passengers are requested to assemble at the muster point on deck level 3 for a lifeboat drill at half past ten. The pool, bars and restaurants will be closed for the duration of the drill. Please ensure that your cabin doors are securely locked and windows or portholes closed during the drill.

4. Speaker 1: How many bags?
    Speaker 2: Just the suitcase to check in. And one piece of hand baggage.
    Speaker 1: Did you pack the case yourself?
    Speaker 2: I did.
    Speaker 1: And could anyone have interfered with the bag since then?

5. Speaker 1: Good evening, sir. How many?
    Speaker 2: Four, but I don't have a reservation.
    Speaker 1: That's no problem. Would you like smoking or no smoking?
    Speaker 2: I don't mind. Actually, would it be possible to seat us on the terrace?

6. I must ask everyone to stay inside the vehicle, and try not to make too much noise. These animals are wild, remember, and can be very dangerous. We've arrived at the busiest time of the day for spotting wildlife, so there's plenty of activity. You can see two hippos on the far side of the water hole, and....

7. Speaker 1: Could you put your seat up please, madam? We're landing shortly.
    Speaker 2: Oh, right.
    Speaker 1: And fold your table away as well. And raise the window blind?

8. Speaker 1: I'd like two for tonight's performance, please.
    Speaker 2: We've got seats in the stalls for £20, or in the circle for £15.
    Speaker 1: Can you see the stage all right from the circle?

9. Your lifejacket is situated under your seat. In the event of an emergency landing on water, place it over your head, and tie the strings around your waist. To inflate it, pull the orange toggle. There is a tube to help keep it fully inflated, a light, and a whistle for attracting attention....

10. Speaker 1: Thank you. What's the fare?
     Speaker 2: That's £8.20.
     Speaker 1: Here's £10. Keep the change.

11. Speaker 1: Summertown, please.
     Speaker 2: Single or return?
     Speaker 1: Return.
     Speaker 2: That's £1.20.
     Speaker 1: Here you are. Could you tell me when we get there please?

12. Speaker 1: A pint of Spitfire and a dry white wine please. Do you serve food?
     Speaker 2: We do. There's a list on the board by the door. Find a table, then give me your order
     when you're ready
     Speaker 1: That's great, thanks.

13. Speaker 1: Excuse me, I asked for well done, and this is rare.
     Speaker 2: I'm sorry, madam. I'll ask the chef to put it under the grill a bit longer.

14. (On a notice): ½ hour: €1. 1 hour: €1.50. Printing; 10C per sheet. Please be careful not to spill food
     or drink on the keyboards. Smoking is strictly prohibited.

15. Directly in front of you are two columns, one with a statue of Saint Mark and one with a statue of
     Saint Theodore. Ahead and on your left is the famous Doge's Palace. Directly to our left is Saint
     Mark's Basilica, and the campanile on your right, which was completely rebuilt after it collapsed, can
     be climbed for a marvellous view of the city.

16. Speaker 1: Day return for one car and five passengers, please.
     Speaker 2: If you leave on the next sailing, that will be £65. It's the peak hour, you see. The sailing
     after that is off-peak and will only cost you £30. You'll have to wait about an hour.
     Speaker 1: OK, we'll take the second sailing. Is there somewhere here we can get a coffee?
     Speaker 2: There's a café on the far side of the harbour.

17. Speaker 1: Two adults and two children please.
     Speaker 2: That's £7 please. Would you like a guide? They're free.
     Speaker 1: Yes please. We're particularly interested in the Egyptian section. Where is that?
     Speaker 2: On this floor, go past the gift shop and the portrait gallery and turn left just before you
     get to the natural history section.

18. Speaker 1: How much do the deckchairs cost?
     Speaker 2: €2 per hour, or €10 for the whole day. Umbrellas are €1 per hour or €5 for the day.

19. Speaker 1: What would you recommend with that, the Chablis or the Riesling?
     Speaker 2: I'll get the sommelier for you sir.
     Speaker 1: Thank you. And could we have some water?
     Speaker 2: Certainly. Still or sparkling?

20. Speaker 1: Please take off your coat and remove all metallic objects from your pocket.
     Speaker 2: And take off my watch?
     Speaker 1: Yes please. You can put everything in one of these trays.

Also see *Where are they 2?* on the next page

Where are they 2?

Look at these extracts from conversations, notices, etc, and decide where you would hear or read each one. Choose from the list in the box. Underline the key words that help you decide your answer.

```
At the airport  •  At a ferry terminal  •  On a bus  •  On a cruise ship
On a sightseeing tour  •  On the beach  •  On an aircraft  •  In a pub or bar
In a hotel  •  In a museum  •  In a restaurant  •  In a taxi
In a theatre  •  In an Internet café
```

1. Hello everyone, this is your captain speaking. Well, we're making good progress despite a strong headwind and yesterday's storm. Sailing conditions are generally much calmer today, but things might get a bit choppy later this evening when we enter the Kalamar Straits. Winds are southerly, force 3 to 4, and there's a good chance...

2. Speaker 1: Window or aisle?
    Speaker 2: Aisle, please.
    Speaker 1: There you are. 25C. Your gate number is 80. Watch the screens for a boarding time.

3. Speaker 1: Good afternoon, madam. Do you have a reservation?
    Speaker 2: Yes, a double for two nights. The name's Gruchy.
    Speaker 1: Thank you, Ms Gruchy. Here's your key. Take the lift to the third floor. The porter will bring your bags.

4. (On a sign) Guests are reminded that they should check out by midday on the day they leave.

5. Speaker 1: How do I get on-line?
    Speaker 2: Well, first of all you need to enter the password we gave you, then click on 'New user', and then double-click on the 'Wannasurf' icon on the left of your screen.

6. Speaker 1: Don't drop that camera: you don't want to get sand in it. And keep it away from the water: if it gets saltwater in it, it'll never work again. And don't leave it lying around in the hot sun. And try not to get any suncream on it.
    Speaker 2: Oh dear, perhaps I should just take it back to the hotel.

7. This is the minibar, and here's the menu and price list. There's a safe in the wardrobe, but we recommend that you leave extremely valuable items in one of the safety deposit boxes at reception. Here's your phone. To get reception, press 0, to get an outside line, press 9. There's a computer internet port by the television, and...

8. Speaker 1: Two bottles of Bud, please.
    Speaker 2: Are you both 18?
    Speaker 1: Yes.
    Speaker 2: I'll need to see some form of ID please.

9. In the unlikely event of a sudden drop in cabin pressure, oxygen masks will automatically drop from the overhead compartments. Pull the mask towards you, fasten it using the strap, and breathe normally. Make sure you own mask is fully attached before helping....

10.	(On the phone)
	Speaker 1: Would you mind making a little less noise, please? It is rather late and the other guests are complaining that they can't sleep.
	Speaker 2: Oh, I'm sorry. Of course we'll keep the noise down.
	Speaker 1: Thank you sir.

11.	Speaker 1: Do you allow children in here?
	Speaker 2; Yes, until seven o'clock. After that, there's a special family room at the back.
	Speaker 1: And do you have a no smoking section?
	Speaker 2: Yes, the family room is no smoking. And we don't allow it at the bar.

12.	Good morning ladies and gentlemen. I'm your captain John Grindon, and together with my first officer Tim Rogers I'll be taking you on the first leg of this flight to Wellington. We're currently waiting for clearance for the tower, and despite a slight delay we won't miss our slot.

13.	Speaker 1: Excuse me, what are all of these extra charges on my bill for?
	Speaker 2: That first one is a $5 cover charge, the second one is a 15% service charge and the third one is an 18% VAT charge.
	Speaker 1: And the fourth one?
	Speaker 2: That's a special $10 charge for the spoon you put in your pocket earlier.

14.	Could I ask everyone to stay together and not to wander off? It can get very busy here at this time of the day. If anyone gets separated from the group, go and wait by the cathedral entrance and I'll come to look for you. We've got a busy itinerary today, so let's get started.

15.	You have a choice of two crossings. There's a normal roll-on-roll-off service at nine o'clock, and a hovercraft service at ten o'clock. The hovercraft is more expensive, but it's much quicker.

16.	Speaker 1: Could you put the meter on please?
	Speaker 2: I'm sorry, it's broken. It doesn't work.
	Speaker 1: In that case, I want you to stop and let me out.
	Speaker 2: Oh, I've just remembered. It does work. I had it fixed this morning. Silly me.

17.	Speaker 1: Please put that back into the display case, madam. We don't allow visitors to touch the exhibits.
	Speaker 2: But it's so beautiful. Whoops, butter fingers, I've dropped it!
	Speaker 1: Oh no! That's a Chin Dynasty vase. It's over fifteen hundred years old.
	Speaker 2: Oh well, at least it wasn't new.

18.	Speaker 1: This is a terrible seat. I can't see the stage very well from here.
	Speaker 2: Well, why don't you ask to change before the curtain goes up?
	Speaker 1: It's already going up. I'll have to wait for the interval now.
	Speaker 3: Shhhh! It's starting.

19.	This place is a fleapit. The air-conditioning doesn't work, I can't open the balcony door, there's a horrible smell coming from the plumbing, the walls are paper-thin, the mattress is lumpy, the sheets are damp, the pillow has mould growing on it and there's a dead cockroach in the wardrobe.

ANSWERS

Several of the answers below are followed by a task for you to do. These tasks are indicated by a ✱ symbol. Try to do them, as they will give you the opportunity to make productive use of the key vocabulary that you have learnt.

Note: AmE = American English (the English used in North America)

Abbreviations 1: International organisations (pages 1 + 2)

Across
4. Hostel   6. Cultural   8. Union   9. Labour   10. Camping   12. Aviation   14. Monetary   17. Tour
18. American   22. Environment   24. Youth   28. Transport   32. Unity   34. Social   35. Standardization
36. Asian   37. Recreation

Down
1. Economic   2. Europe   3. Hotel   4. Health   5. Tourism   7. Trade   11. Agencies   13. Airports
15. South   16. Travel   19. Convention   20. Federation   21. Reconstruction   23. Independent
25. Operators   26. Development   27. Automobile   29. Shipping   30. Africa   31. Industry   33. Pacific

✱ Choose three or four organisations from this exercise that you are familiar with, and write a brief description of what they do, how they function, who benefits from them, their role in international travel and tourism, etc. Alternatively, choose some organisations from your own country or region, and describe them.

Abbreviations 2 (pages 3 + 4)

1. ETA: estimated time of arrival   2. F & B: food and beverage   3. PNR: passenger name record   4. FAA: Federal Aviation Administration   5. CCTV: closed-circuit television   6. RTW: round the world   7. CSQ: customer survey questionnaire   8. HAG: have-a-go (an idiomatic expression)   9. BYO: bring your own (customers are allowed to bring their own alcohol to a restaurant - either offered as a cost-saving incentive for the customer, or used when a restaurant doesn't have a licence to sell alcohol. The fee a restaurant charges the customer for opening the bottle is called *corkage*)   10. ETD: estimated time of departure   11. LRV: light refreshment voucher   12. CRS: computer reservation system (also known as *central reservation system*)   13. APEX: Advance Purchase Excursion (an APEX fare is an especially cheap air fare which must be booked a certain time before the date of departure - usually 1 - 4 weeks - and allows a stay of a certain length - usually more than one week and less than six)   14. B & B: bed and breakfast   15. POS: point of sale   16. OW: one way (also called a *single* in British English) / RT: round trip (also called a *return* in British English)   17. PRO: Public Relations Officer   18. RRP: recommended retail price   19. ASAP: as soon as possible (also written *a.s.a.p.*)   20. VIP: very important person   21. 4WD: 4-wheel drive (we also say *SUV: sport utility vehicle*)   22. GMT: Greenwich Mean Time   23. IDD: International Direct Dialling   24. FFP: frequent flyer programme   25. ATM: automated teller machine (the trade name *Cashpoint* is often used in the UK, and we also say *cash machine*)   26. EHO: Environmental Health Officer   27. ESA: environmentally sensitive area (conservation areas defined by the EU)   28. FET: foreign escorted tour   29. GDS: global distribution system (also known as a *global reservation system*. These can also be used for hotel reservations, car rental, etc)   30. HQ: headquarters   31. E: electronic   32. ZIP: Zone Improvement Plan (spoken as one word. A *ZIP code* is called a *postcode* in British English)   33. ROI: return on investment (also called *return on capital*)   34. EST: Eastern Standard Time / PST: Pacific Standard Time / MST: Mountain Standard Time / CST: Central Standard Time / AST: Atlantic Standard Time (there is also an *Alaskan Standard Time*) / PST   35. DST: daylight saving time

Abbreviations 3: Holiday brochure (page 5)

pp = per person   pw = per week   incl = including   VAT = Value Added Tax (a tax, common in all EU countries, imposed as a percentage of the invoice value of goods and services)   SC = self-catering   B & B = bed and breakfast HB = half-board   FB = full board   AI = all-inclusive (for more information on these abbreviations, see the exercise on *Accommodation types and tariffs*)   n/a = not available *or* not applicable   apt = apartments   TV = television IDD = International Direct Dialling   k = kitchen   b = bathroom   wc = toilet (= *water closet*, a formal expression) priv = private   a/c = air conditioning   locn = location   nr = near   mins =- minutes   est = estimated   hrs = hours GF = ground floor   1F = first floor   2F = second floor   min = minimum   nts = nights   bkgs = bookings chq = cheque   flts = flights   dep = depart   wkly = weekly   Sat = Saturday   a.m. = before noon (= *ante meridiem*) Wed = Wednesday   p.m. = after noon (= *post meridiem*)   Apr = April   Jul = July   PLC = public limited company mbr = member   ATOL = Air Travel Organiser's Licence (a British licence which has to be held by any company or person offering package holidays or charter flights, and includes a bond to protect travellers if the company goes into liquidation)   ABTA = Association of British Travel Agents (a British bonding scheme designed to protect or compensate travellers if, for example, the tour operator goes into liquidation while the traveller is on holiday)   IATA = International Air Transport Association (an organization which regulates international air travel)   IIP = Investors in People (a British organization: IIP members continually work to improve the quality of their staff so that they provide a better quality of service)   FOC = Friends of Conservation (an environmental protection and support group)   TC = traveller's cheques

Accommodation types and tariffs (pages 6 + 7)

Exercise 1: (these are the most appropriate answers)
1. villa   2. chalet   3. apartment   4. guest house (also called a *bed and breakfast*, or *B and B*: see note after Exercise 3)
5. boutique hotel (these are usually small-to-medium size hotels, very modern, very fashionable, in interesting buildings, and with excellent service)   6. motel (sometimes called a *motor hotel*, *motor inn* or *travel hotel*)   7. hotel garni
8. hostel (sometimes called a *youth hostel*)   9. commercial hotel (sometimes called a *transit hotel*) 10. apartment hotel
11. luxury hotel   12. tourist hotel

Many countries have accommodation for travellers and tourists that is unique or special to that country. For example, *Gasthaus* or *Gasthof* in Germany, *parador* in Spain, *pousada* in Portugal, *pension* in France, *ryokan* in Japan, *rest house* or *dormhouse* in India, etc.

Exercise 2:
1. king size   2. suite (varieties of these include a *junior suite*, a *honeymoon suite*, a *presidential suite*, etc)
3. bunk bed (sometimes just called a *bunk*)   4. twin (a room with <u>three</u> small beds is called a *triple*)   5. single
6. sofa bed   7. Murphy (a trade name. Other types of bed which can be stored during the day to create extra room include *rollaways* and *Z-beds*)   8. double   9. dormitory   10. en suite   11. studio room   12. family room

Exercise 3:
A (You pay for the room only):
European plan (EP)   self-catering (SC) (this expression is usually used when travellers stay in villas, chalets, apartment hotels or self-contained accommodation on resorts. The accommodation in these places usually includes cooking facilities, with plates, cups, cutlery, etc provided by the owners)
B (you pay for the room and breakfast)
Bed and breakfast (often abbreviated to *BB* or *B and B*)*   Bermuda Plan (BP) (this includes a *full English* or *American breakfast*, which consists - among other things - of cereal, bacon or ham, eggs, toast or waffles with tea or coffee)
Continental Plan (CP) (this includes a *Continental breakfast* of bread, croissants, pastries, etc, with coffee)
C (you pay for the room and two meals)
Demi pension   half board (HB)   Modified American Plan (MAP)
D (you pay for the room and three meals)
American plan (AP)   bed and board   full board (FB)   en pension
E (you pay for the room, all meals and snacks, and drinks)
all-inclusive (AI) (specific to package holidays in hotels or resorts. All-inclusive holidays also include flights, transfers, taxes, etc)

* In the United Kingdom and North America, *Bed and Breakfast* also refers to a private house which provides accommodation and breakfast for travellers and tourists. They are very popular, mainly because they can often be found in places which don't have larger hotels, and also because they are considerably cheaper than staying in hotels.

If customers book a hotel room during the *busy season* or *peak period*, they usually have to pay the *rack rate* (the advertised price for the room), but if they book *in advance* or *out of season* (when the hotel is quieter), they may get a *discount* (and therefore pay less).

When hotel charges are calculated on the basis of two people sharing a room, a single person travelling as part of a group might be required to pay a *single room supplement* for *single occupancy*. This is an extra charge on top of what he is already paying. For example, if *two* people sharing a room pay $40 each, then *one* person using a similar room might pay $50 (= $40 + a *single room supplement* of $10).

> ✱ Think of the accommodation you have stayed in when you have travelled on holiday or on business. What sort of accommodation was it? What sort of rooms did it have? What tariffs could you choose to pay? Write a brief description of three or four places you have stayed in.

Note: *accommodation* cannot be plural in British English, but it can be plural (*accommodations*) in American English.

Airline terminology (pages 8 + 9)

Across:
2. reissue (this can also be a noun: a *reissue*) (alternatively, if the route remains the same, a ticket can be *revalidated* so that it can be used on another date: a sticker is attached to the original ticket to indicate this)   7. bumping (this usually happens when an airline has overbooked)   9. carrier   11. stopover (passengers on a stopover usually spend a day or two in the stopover city)   14. published (a carrier's version of an *RRP* - a *recommended retail price*)   15. first (a fare code is also called a *booking code*) 17. compensation   18. sharing   20. cancellation (sometimes called a *cancellation penalty*)   21. electronic (also known as *e-tickets*. The piece of paper passengers receive via their email when they book a flight is a receipt, and not the actual ticket for the flight)   25. transferable   26. locator   29. club
31. connecting   32. penalty (and if a passenger cancels his booking, he won't receive all of his money back)   33. direct (note that a *direct flight* is <u>not</u> the same as a *non-stop flight*. Direct flight passengers may or may not be allowed off the aircraft during the first landing)

ANSWERS *(cont.)*

Down:
1. leg (sometimes also called a *segment*)   3. standby   4. layover (a layover often involves waiting at an airport *overnight* for a connecting flight)   5. coach   6. business   8. non-stop   10. overbooking   12. allowance   13. peak   16. availability (note that availability refers only to seats *at a certain price*, and does not indicate the total number of free seats on the flight)   19. endorsable   21. economy (note that there are lots of other class codes, depending on how much the passenger has paid, whether the ticket is refundable or transferable, etc. These vary from airline to airline)   22. connection   23. show   24. promotional   27. capacity (the number of capacity-controlled fares may be increased if seats sell slowly, or decreased if they sell quickly)   28. confirmed   30. circle

> ✱ Look at the expressions in the exercise, and the answers and other information above, then close your book and try to write down as many of the words and expressions as you can remember. Then look at each word / expression you have written down and try to explain what it means.

At the airport (pages 10 + 11)

1. transit (expressions with *transit* include: transit *lounge*; transit *visa*; *to be in transit*)   2. terminal (also called a *terminal building*. Note that an *air terminal* is a building in a town where passengers meet to be taken by bus or train to an airport outside town)   3. disembark   4. arrivals (also: *arrivals hall, arrivals lounge*)   5. Gate   6. security   7. charter (also a verb: *to charter*. Aircraft are often chartered by several tour companies in a *split charter* arrangement. If these flights are regular over a fixed period of time they are called *series charters*. When just one tour company uses the aircraft over a fixed period of time, this is called a *time charter*. If an aircraft is chartered for one flight only, this is called an *ad hoc charter*)   8. Bagtrack   9. domestic (the opposite is *international*. Many airports have *domestic terminals* for flights within the country)   10. slots   11. landing   12. checked (also called *hold baggage*. The baggage that a passenger takes onto the aircraft himself is called *hand baggage* or *unchecked baggage*)   13. boarding   14. runway (before it reaches the runway the aircraft moves along a *taxiway*. The verb is *to taxi*)   15. duty (note that passengers flying between European Union countries cannot buy *duty free* products, but they <u>can</u> buy *tax free* products)   16. apron (also called a *stand*)   17. control   18. clearance   19. airbridge (when passengers take a bus to the aircraft and board using steps, this is called a *remote stand*)   20. Passengers'   21. Federal (in the USA. The British equivalent is the *CAA*: the *Civil Aviation Authority*)   22. excess (this is also used to describe the money passengers have to pay to take this baggage on the aircraft: '*I had to pay almost £200 excess baggage.*')   23. carousel   24. airside (the area before security, etc, is called the *landside*)   25. Transport (an organisation which regulates international air travel)   26. holding (this is an area between the apron and the runway)   27. claim (also called *reclaim*)   28. codes

The words in the shaded vertical strip are: *Immigration control** and *customs*.

**Immigration control* is also called *passport control*.

At the hotel (page 12)

1. business centre (or conference centre) / ADSL (= *asymmetric digital subscriber line*) connection (or wireless connection) / tea and coffee making facilities (also found in some hotel rooms)   2. room service (which provides food and drink) / housekeeping (which is responsible for cleaning the rooms, running the hotel *laundry*, etc)   3. airport transfer (usually by minibus or *limo* (= *limousine*))   4. rack rate / reservation (the verb is *to reserve*. We also say *to book* or *make a booking*) / vacancies   5. check-out time   6. honeymoon suite / Presidential suite   7. reception / check in / registration card (the verb is *to register*) / key card / lift (elevator = AmE)   8. minibar / tariff (we also say *price list*) / safe (or safety deposit box) / direct-dial telephone / balcony / pay-TV   9. bar / restaurant / (swimming) pool / residents / non-residents

Basic foods (pages 13 + 14)

<u>Meat and poultry</u>: bacon / beef / chicken / duck / goose / hare / lamb / mutton / pheasant / pigeon / pork / rabbit / veal / venison
<u>Fish and seafood</u>: cod / crab / crayfish / haddock / herring / lobster / mussel / oyster / plaice / prawn / scallop / salmon / trout / tuna
<u>Vegetables</u>: artichoke / asparagus / aubergine (also called *eggplant*) / broccoli / cabbage / carrot / cauliflower / courgette / cucumber / lettuce / marrow / mushroom / onion / peas / pepper (also called a *capsicum*, *bell pepper*, or *red* / *green* / *yellow pepper*) / pumpkin / sweetcorn / turnip

Note that some of the foods classified under vegetables above are technically fruits, bulbs or squashes, so *vegetable* is used here as a general term to describe how they are normally prepared and / or eaten.

<u>Fruits</u>: apricot / cherry / gooseberry / grape / kiwi (also called *kiwifruit* or *Chinese gooseberry*) / lime / lychee / mango / nectarine / plum / pear / papaya (also called *pawpaw*) / pineapple / strawberry / watermelon
<u>Herbs and spices</u>: chilli (also spelt *chile*) / cinnamon / coriander (called *cilantro* in AmE) / cumin / garlic / ginger / nutmeg / oregano / pepper / paprika / parsley / rosemary / saffron / sage / turmeric / thyme
<u>Other basic foods</u>: beans / bread / cereal / cheese / cream / eggs / lentils / margarine / noodles / oil / olives / pasta / rice / yoghurt

British and American English (page 15)

1. angry = mad   2. cinema = theater (or *movie theater*)   film = movies   3. porter = bellhop (or *bellboy*)   anywhere = anyplace   4. taxi = cab   5. sweets = candy (or *candies*)   biscuits = cookies   crisps = chips (or *potato chips*)   ill = sick   6. ground = first   first = second   lift = elevator   7. holiday = vacation   autumn = fall   8. chemist = drugstore   shop = store   trousers = pants   9. bill = check   10. note = bill   10. single = one-way   return = round-trip   11. car = automobile   crossroads = intersection   roundabout = traffic circle   lights = signal   flyover = overpass   motorway = freeway   puncture = flat   diversion = detour   petrol = gas   12. underground = subway   pavement = sidewalk   subway = underpass

Note that there are several words which can have different meanings in British English and American English. For example, in British English, *chips* are fried strips of potato which are eaten hot; in the USA *chips* are fried slices of potato eaten cold out of a bag (hot fried strips of potato in the USA are called *fries*). Some other examples include: *bill*, *mad*, *biscuit* (the American word for a *scone*), *first / second / third* (etc) *floor*, *holiday* (a public day of celebration in the USA, e.g., Thanksgiving, Christmas, Presidents' Day), *pants*, *gas*, *subway*.

Also note that there are some spelling differences. These include:
Words which end in *-gue* in British English only end with *-g* in American English (*dialogue = dialog, catalogue = catalog*, etc)
Words which end with *-re* in British English end with *-er* in American English (*theatre = theater, centre = center*, etc)
British-English words which use a double *l* in unstressed syllables only use a single *l* in American English (*traveller = traveler, levelling = leveling*, etc)
Words which end in *-our* in British English only end with *-or* in American English (*colour = color, flavour = flavor*, etc)
Words which end with *-ise* or *-ize* in British-English can only end in *-ize* in American-English (*realise / realize = realize* only, etc)

Other vocabulary differences include:
aeroplane (BrE) = airplane (AmE)   caravan (BrE) = trailer (AmE)   flat (BrE) = apartment (AmE)   grilled (BrE) = broiled (AmE)   nappy (BrE) = diaper (AmE)   post (BrE) = mail (AmE)   postcode (BrE) = zip code (AmE)   pub (BrE) = bar (AmE)   public toilet (BrE) = restroom (AmE)   rubbish (BrE) = trash (AmE)   torch (BrE) = flashlight (AmE)

British people usually understand American-English words, but Americans do not always understand British-English words. People in Australia and New Zealand tend to use British-English rather than American-English words.

Currencies (pages 16 + 17)

Exercise 1:
1. Singapore Dollar / Singapore   2. Baht / Thailand   3. Kuwait Dinar / Kuwait   4. Indian Rupee / India
5. Swiss Franc / Switzerland   6. Yuan / China   7. Pound Sterling / United Kingdom (£)   8. Rouble / Russia
9. Dong / Vietnam   10. Bolivar / Venezuela   11. Hong Kong Dollar / Hong Kong   12. Cyprus Pound / Cyprus*
13. Won / Republic of Korea (usually referred to as *South Korea*)**   14. US Dollar / United States of America (US$)
15. Chilean Peso / Chile   16. Iranian Rial / Iran   17. Egyptian Pound / Egypt   18. Yen / Japan (¥)   19. Saudi Arabian Riyal / Saudi Arabia   20. Australian Dollar / Australia   21. UAE Dirham / United Arab Emirates   22. Real / Brazil
23. Czech Koruna / Czech Republic   24. Jordanian Dinar / Jordan   25. Maltese Lira / Malta

* The Cyprus Pound is used in the southern part of the (currently) divided island. North Cyprus uses the *Turkish Lira* (TRL).
* * The Won is the name of the currency used in both South Korea and North Korea (known formally as the *Democratic People's Republic of Korea*). The currency code for the North Korean Won is *KPW*.

Note that some countries (especially those with 'soft' currencies) use or accept more than one currency. Cuba, for example, uses three currencies: the Cuban Peso, the Convertible Peso (1 Peso = US$1) and the US Dollar.

Exercise 2:
1. Ecuador   2. Israel   3. Estonia   4. South Africa   5. Lithuania   6. Latvia   7. Slovenia   8. Romania
9. Pakistan (the Pakistani Rupee)   10. Peru   11. Bangladesh   12. Nicaragua   13. Ukraine   14. Indonesia
15. Malaysia

Exercise 3: (*these countries, territories, etc, were all using the Euro in March 2005*):
Austria, Belgium, Finland, France, French Guiana, Guadeloupe, Martinique, Mayotte, Monaco, Réunion, St Pierre,

ANSWERS *(cont.)*

Miquelon, Germany, Greece, Irish Republic, Italy, San Marino, Luxembourg, Netherlands, Portugal, Spain, Andorra, Spanish North Africa.

Euro is sometimes written *euro*.

> ✺ Think of 10 essential items (eg milk, petrol, etc), and 10 luxury items (e.g., DVD player, a meal in a nice restaurant, etc). Make a list of these, then write down the prices you might expect to pay for them in your country or city. If you are using this book in a class with other students from other countries, make your list of items together as a class, then write down the prices individually, and finally compare your prices with the others in your class. Is there a big difference between prices for the same items?

Documents and paperwork (pages 18 + 19)

1. transit visa   2. landing card   3. ticket (*round-trip = return* in British English. A ticket that is valid for one direction only is called a *one-way* ticket in American English and a *single* in British English)   4. boarding pass (also called a *boarding card*)   5. hotel voucher   6. travel voucher (also called a *Miscellaneous Charges Order*, or *MCO*)   7. Form E111   8. travel insurance   9. passport / application form (you can *fill in*, *fill out* or *complete* an application form)   10. flight coupon   11. rental agreement / driving licence   12. ID (identity) card   13. work permit (also called an *employment permit*, or - in the USA - a *green card*. In Britain, a green card is an insurance certificate to prove that a car is insured for travel abroad)   14. certificate of airworthiness / certificate of seaworthiness   15. clearance certificate   16. vaccination certificate / health declaration form   17. Property Irregularity Report (PIR) / baggage check   18. food hygiene certificate   19. Customer Satisfaction Questionnaire (CSQ)   20. claim form   21. receipt   22. docket   23. revalidation sticker   24. multiple entry visa   25. exit visa

Others include:
Bill of exchange / bill of lading / Certificate of origin / certificate of registration / e-ticket / food voucher / hotel licence / medical certificate

Employment (page 20)

1. employers   2. employees   3. salaries (a *salary* is usually paid monthly by cheque or direct payment to the employee's bank account. A *wage* is usually paid daily or weekly, often in cash. Wages are usually paid for *temporary* and / or *unskilled* or *semi-skilled* work)   4. minimum wage   5. rewards   6. benefits (a job usually offers a *rewards package*, or a *rewards and benefits package*, to its employees: this is what the employee receives in return for working for the company, and includes the salary, also formally called the *remuneration*)   7. leave (a formal word for holiday)   8. equal opportunities (called *affirmative recruitment* in the USA)   9. discrimination   10. work permit (also called a *work visa*. In the USA it is called a *green card*)   11. full-time   12. part-time   13. contract   14. duties   15. fixed (= a *fixed-term contract*)   16. open-ended (it has no fixed finishing period. Some contracts are also *permanent*.)   17. casual (casual work is usually unskilled or semi-skilled)   18. on call (= available for work)   19. report (answer to = less formal)   20. seasonal   21. peak   22. permanent   23. front-of-house   24. shift   25. morning shift   26. afternoon shift   27. night shift (also informally called the *graveyard shift*. Evening shifts are sometimes referred to as the *twilight shift*)   28. Back-of-house   29. flexitime (= *flexible working time*)   30. core-time (most flexitime systems have some core-time, where employees have to be at work)   31. split-shift (also informally called a *bookend shift*)   32. allowed time (= free time)   33. break   34. overtime   35. double time (when the employee receives twice his / her usual payment)   36. short-handed (we also say under-staffed)   37. application   38. interview   39. personnel   40. experience

Environmental and conservation issues (pages 21 + 22)

Exercise 1:
1. mass   2. degradation   3. resources   4. depleted   5. deforestation   6. erosion   7. wildlife   8. habitats   9. pollution   10. fossil fuels   11. depletion   12. ozone layer   13. acid rain   14. global warming   15. waste   16. natural   17. overcrowded   18. ecosystems   19. impact   20. audits   21. World Heritage   22. biosphere reserves   23. Environmentally Sensitive   24. Special Protection   25. Blue Flag   26. Green Globe   27. energy management   28. Greenpeace   29. ecotourism   30 / 31. sustainable / responsible (in either order)

Exercise 2:
1. recycled   2. subsidise   3. endangered   4. damage   5. protect   6. Earth   7. Kyoto   8. organic   9. genetically (*genetically modified* is often abbreviated to *GM*)   10. conserve

> ✺ Imagine that you work for a travel company that is concerned about the negative impact that tourism has on the environment. What advice would you give customers using your services so that they adapt a 'greener' and more responsible way of travelling?

Food issues (pages 23 + 24)

Exercise 1:
1. vegetarian / vegan   2. health / moral / religion   3. allergic / allergy / anaphylactic (the most common *allergy-inducing* foods include *strawberries*, *eggs*, *milk*, *cereals*, *peas*, *nuts* and *shellfish*)   4. intolerant / intolerance (a food intolerance is similar to an allergy, but not as severe)   5. analysis / control / hygiene (the adjective is *hygienic*. The opposite of hygienic

is *unhygienic*) / environmental (abbreviated to *EHO*)   6. steaming / minerals / vitamins / frying (frying expressions include *shallow frying, deep frying, stir frying, griddle frying*. The adjective is *fried*) / boiling / roasting (Meat and some vegetables can be *roasted*. Bread and cakes are *baked*) / grilling**   7. halal / kosher   8. rare / medium / medium-rare / well-done / raw / blue (food which is not cooked enough is *undercooked*, food which is cooked too much is *overcooked*. Food which has been overcooked so that it has gone black is *burnt*)   9. organic / free-range / additives (*monosodium glutamate* is abbreviated to *MSG*) / E-numbers*   10. diet / cut down on / give up / calories / fibre / fat (other food properties include: *protein*, *calcium*, *carbohydrates*, *cholesterol*)

Exercise 2:
1. contaminated / bacteria / Salmonella / food poisoning (*Escherichia coli* is often abbreviated to E. Coli)   2. use-by date / stale / mould (the adjective is *mouldy*)   3. sell-by date (some foods also have a *best-before date*, which means that they can be consumed *after* that date, but might not be so good)   4. sour / gone off   5. rotten   6. rancid
7. undercooked

* A lot of people also try to avoid *genetically modified* (*GM*) foods because they think they might be unsafe.

** Other words describing the preparation of food include:
blanch / braise / caramelise / carve / chill / chop / dice / flambé / flavour / fricassee / garnish / grate / grind / liquidize / marinade / mix / parboil / peel / poach / sauté / season / simmer / slice / stir / strain / stuff / warm

Geography and geographical features (pages 25 + 26)

A.
1. city   county   country   continent   (*tributary* does not belong here)
2. footpath   track   lane   road   (*peak* does not belong here)
3. hillock   hill   mountain   range (=group of mountains)   (*shore* does not belong here)
4. tree   copse   wood   forest   (*beach* does not belong here)
5. pond   lake   sea   ocean   (*cape* does not belong here)
6. hollow   gorge   valley   plain   (*waterfall* does not belong here)
7. inlet   cove   bay   gulf   (*ridge* does not belong here)
8. brook   stream   river   estuary   (*cliff* does not belong here)

B.
Geographical features associated with water and the sea:
coast   peninsula   shore   beach   cape   source   coastline   tributary   waterfall   mouth   cliff   (coral) reef   tide   wave
Geographical features associated with land, hills and mountains:
mountainous   ridge   cliff   summit   glacier   plateau   peak   highlands   desert
Words associated with agriculture and rural land:
depopulation   fertile   under-developed   vegetation   irrigation
Words associated with towns and cities:
urban sprawl densely-populated industrialised conurbation overcrowding pollution capital congestion cosmopolitan

C.
1. capital   2. densely-populated   3. industrialised   4. urban sprawl   5. city   6. irrigation   7. source   8. peaks
9. range   10. depopulation   11. Valley   12. waterfalls   13. streams   14. lane   15. track   16. Ocean   17. cape / peninsula   18. hills   19. plain   20. mouth   21. fertile   22. waves   23. shore / beach   24. country

Specific geographical and geo-political names commonly used in the travel and tourism industry include:

The Amazon / the Americas (North America / South America / Latin America) / the Arctic / Antarctica / the Balkans / the Baltic States / Benelux / the Caribbean / the Near East / the Middle East / the Far East / the Gulf States / the Pacific Rim / Scandinavia / the West Indies / the South Pacific / the United Kingdom / the British isles / Asia / South Asia / South-East Asia / Australasia / the Antipodes / Europe / Africa

> ✻ Imagine that a visitor to your country or region has asked you to describe it to them before they arrive so that they know what to expect. Use the key vocabulary from the exercises to write a description.

Holiday activities and equipment (pages 27 + 28)

Exercise 1:
1. sightseeing   2. bungee jumping   3. fishing / deep-sea fishing   4. swimming (when we use a mask and a snorkel to see underwater, we often call this *snorkelling*)   5. sunbathing (*flip-flops* = British English; *thongs* = American English)
6. scuba diving (*scuba* = **s**elf-**c**ontained **u**nderwater **b**reathing **a**pparatus. PADI = **P**rofessional **A**ssociation of **D**iving **I**nstructors. *Buddy* is an informal word for a *friend* or *partner*)   7. jeep safari (*RV* = *recreational vehicle*. Also called an *SUV* = *sport utility vehicle*)   8. walking / hiking (hiking tends to involve walking on rough ground, e.g., in mountains or forests, and over longer distances. *Trekking* can also be used for very long hikes that last a few days or longer. Hiking and trekking are known as *tramping* in New Zealand)   9. tennis   10. golf   11. rock or mountain climbing   12. sailing
13. skiing (the speaker has forgotten to mention his *skis*)   14. cycling (when this is done on rough ground, we often call

69

it *mountain biking*)   15. eating out   16. clubbing (*the early hours* = very late at night / very early in the morning)
17. photography (*SLR = single lens reflex*, a type of camera. *Point-and-shoot* describes any camera which is very easy to use)

Note that the verb which precedes activities ending with -*ing* is go (I'm **going skiing** this winter, Last year we **went** scuba **diving** in the Red Sea, Let's **go surfing** now). Other sports use the verb play (Do you **play golf**? We're going to **play volleyball**.)

Exercise 2:
1. goggles   2. helmet   3. sandals (or *flip flops*, if they are made of rubber)   4. suncream (suncream can be *low factor* or *high factor*. If it is *high factor*, it provides your skin with more protection)   5. waterproofs (*waterproof* is the adjective: a *waterproof coat*)   6. flippers   7. boots   8. tackle   9. life jacket (also called a *life preserver* in American English)   10. rubber ring (compare this with a *lifebelt*, which is carried on ships and boats and used in emergencies: *There weren't enough lifebelts for everyone on the boat*. A lifebelt is also called a *life preserver* in American English)
11. walkie-talkie   12. wetsuit   13. gloves   14. a map (an *atlas* is a book of maps)

> ✹ Look at the activities which weren't described, and make a list of the equipment, etc, that is needed for each one. Can you think of any other holiday activities, and the equipment you would need to do them?

Idioms 1 (pages 29 + 30)

1. B   2. A (derived from the expression *road rage*, where drivers suddenly get angry because of the way other people behave on the road)   3. C   4. C   5. A (this is a derogatory expression. We also say *tourist enclaves*, which is less derogatory)   6. C   7. B (if a place is *very* dirty, we can describe it as a *pigsty*)   8. B (there are lots of idiomatic expressions for stomach ache caused by poor hygiene, most of them used humorously. Examples include: *travellers' trots*; *Montezuma's revenge, gippy tummy*)   9. A   10. C (we can also say *off the map* or *in the back of beyond*)   11. C
12. B   13. B   14. B   15. A   16. A   17. A (also *off the tourist track*)   18. C   19. C   20. B   21. C   22. A (this can also be a verb: *to rip somebody off*)   23. B   24. B   25. A (we also call this a *jolly*: 'We're going on a jolly to Frankfurt.')

Idioms 2 (pages 31 + 32)

(A, B, C, etc, indicates which paragraph the idiom can be found in)
1. get your money's worth (E)   2. out of the question (D)   3. dog-tired (F)   4. out of this world (F)
5. shop around (C)   6. a pick-up joint (A)   7. nicked (D) (we also say *pinched* or *swiped*)   8. slept like a log (F) (when you fall asleep very quickly, you can say that you *went out like a light*)   9. went out of their way / fell over himself (F) (we can also say *bent over backwards* or *moved heaven and earth*)   10. in good hands (F)   11. natives (E)   12. misery guts (B)   13. gone to the dogs (B) (we can also say *gone to rack and ruin* or *gone downhill*)   14. bucket shop (C)   15. a stone's throw (A)   16. grub (E)   17. take the skin off your teeth (E)   18. stormed out (D)   19. pulling a fast one (A) (we can also say *trying one on*)   20. a tough customer (D)   21. brought prices down (C)   22. laying down the law (B)
23. an unearthly hour (C) (we can also say *at an ungodly hour*, or *at the crack of dawn*)   24. flew off the handle (D) (we can also say *threw her toys out of the pram* or *threw a wobbly*)   25. picking holes in everything (D)   26. wasn't really up to the mark (B) (we can also say *wasn't up to scratch* or *didn't come up to scratch*)   27. fell short of my expectations (B)   28. pay through the nose (B) (we can also say *pay an arm and a leg*)   29. read between the lines (A)   30. keep the noise down (F)   31. plonk (E)   32. pull his socks up (D)   33. cut price (C) / cheap'n'cheerful (E)   34. a good deal (C)
35. in the back of beyond (A) (we can also say *off the map* or *in the middle of nowhere*)   36. round the houses (C)
37. skipper (D)   38. steep (C) (if something is so expensive that you cannot afford it, we say it is *prohibitive*)

In the air (pages 33 + 34)

Exercise 1:
1. first officer   2. subsonic   3. dry lease (if the crew, fuel and other provisions are included, it is called a *wet lease*)
4. narrow body   5. wide body   6. turboprops   7. Club   8. flight deck (called a *cockpit* on small aircraft, and sometimes called *the office* by pilots)   9. stacking   10. helicopter   11. aisle   12. cabin crew (also called *flight attendants*)   13. air taxis   14. long-haul (the opposite is *short-haul*)   15. coach   16. executive (*executive* is an adjective that is often used to describe something that is better than usual, for example, *executive service, executive class, executive lounge*, etc)

The expression in the shaded vertical strip is *Oneworld alliance*.

Exercise 2:
Add-Collect (also called *Additional Collection*) / Add-on fare / Advance Purchase Fare (or APEX) / airline designator* (for example, BA = British Airways, JL = Japan Airlines, etc) / airport code (for example, LHR = London Heathrow, ORY = Paris Orly, etc) / airport tax / base fare / blackout period / change of equipment / city pair / commuter affiliate / conditional fare / double booking (also called *duplicate booking*) / fare basis code / gateway city / grounded / hub / interline connection / lowest fare / lowest available fare / maximum stay / minimum stay / minimum connecting time / offline connection / open ticket / open-jaw ticket or trip / passenger facility charge (PFC) / point to point / prepaid ticket advice (PTA) / re-route / restricted-to-airport check-in / Saturday night stay / unrestricted fare

*Note that IATA designators have *two* letters, and ICAO designators have *three* letters (for example, British Airways has the IATA designator *BA*, and the ICAO designator *BAW*)

Money matters (pages 35 + 36)

Exercise 1:
1. cash   2. hard currency   3. soft currencies   4. strong   5. weak   6. traveller's cheques   7. bureau de change
8. exchange rate   9. commission   10. transaction   11. debit card   12. advance   13. credit card   14. interest
15. in the black (= *in credit*)   16. in the red (= *overdrawn*)   17. credit limit

Exercise 2:
1. bankrupt (also: *goes broke*, *goes into liquidation*, or *goes into receivership*)   2. refund   3. rack rate
4. discount   5. group rate   6. single supplement (some hotels charge guests for lending them things such as safety deposit boxes, irons, cots for babies, etc. This is called a *supplementary charge*)   7. recommended retail price (abbreviated to *RRP*. Also *MRP*: *manufacturer's retail price*)   8. haggle (= (*informal*) to argue about the price of something in a shop so that you get a good price)   9 / 10 / 11. good deal / bargain / special price (in any order, but *special price* is the best answer for number 10)   12. overpriced   13. overcharged   14 / 15. kickback / backhander (in either order. These are both informal words for an unofficial, sometimes illegal, commission)   16. compensation (also a verb: *to compensate*)

Exercise 3:
1. inclusive   2. VAT (value added tax)   3. service   4. maintenance   5. Duty (a tax paid in the UK by air passengers. It varies in amount depending on the passenger's destination and the class of travel)*   6. penalty   7. surcharge
8. backward pricing   9. price cutting   10. price discrimination (also called *differential pricing*)   11. predatory pricing
12. commission   13. fee-based pricing   14. cost-plus

*Other taxes include:
bed tax   departure tax   entry tax   exit tax   hotel tax   room tax   sales tax   security tax

Nationalities (page 37)

1. Afghan   2. Argentinean   3. Australian   4. Belgian   5. Brazilian   6. Canadian   7. Chilean   8. Chinese
9. Cuban   10. Cypriot   11. Czech   12. Danish   13. Egyptian   14. Finnish   15. French   16. Greek   17. Chinese
18. Indian   19. Iranian   20. Iraqi   21. Japanese   22. Jordanian   23. Kazakh   24. Kenyan   25. Kuwaiti
26. Laotian   27. Libyan   28. Maltese   29. Moroccan   30. Burmese   31. Nepalese   32. Dutch   33. New Zealand
34. Norwegian   35. Oman   36. Peruvian   37. Filipino   38. Russian   39. Saudi   40. Singaporean   41. Slovakian
42. Korean   43. Spanish   44. Sudanese   45. Swedish   46. Swiss   47. Syrian   48. Thai   49. Turkish   50. Ukrainian
51. British*   52. American   53. Venezuelan   54. Vietnamese   55. Yemeni   56. Zimbabwean

* The *United Kingdom* consists of four 'countries': *England*, *Wales*, *Scotland* and *Northern Ireland*. A lot of people like to proclaim their national individuality by calling themselves *English*, *Welsh*, *Scottish* or *Irish* instead of British. *Great Britain* is the name given to England, Scotland and Wales but <u>not</u> Northern Ireland. *The British Isles* is a geographical name for the region that includes Great Britain, Northern Ireland and the Republic of Ireland.
Note that the nationality for *Scotland* is *Scottish*, and not *Scotch* (which is the name given to the drink). A person who comes from Scotland is a *Scot*.

> ✸ What do you know about the countries in this exercise? Do you know the names of their capital or principal cities, the language(s) spoken, principal religion(s), well-known geographical features, famous sights, what their economy is based on, etc? Choose some of these countries and write a brief paragraph about each one.

On the road (pages 38 + 39)

1. motorway   /   freeway or expressway (expressways usually run through or around cities)
2. toll road   /   turnpike (a bridge that you have to pay to cross is called a *toll bridge*)
3. ring road (also called a *by-pass*)
4. scenic route
5. bonnet = hood / boot = trunk / diversion = detour / dual carriageway = divided highway / flyover = overpass / indicator = turn signal / junction = intersection (a junction where four roads meet is called a crossroads in British English) / main road = highway / pavement (for pedestrians) = sidewalk / petrol = gas / puncture = flat / roundabout = traffic circle / subway (for pedestrians to walk under a road) = underpass / taxi = cab / traffic lights = traffic signal / tyre = tire / verge = shoulder (in Britain, the emergency stopping lane on a motorway is called the *hard shoulder*) / windscreen = windshield / wing = fender
6. licence / insurance / road tax (People who are learning to drive have a *provisional* driving licence, people who have passed their test have a *full* driving licence. Drivers put a *tax disc* on the windscreen of their car to show that they have paid road tax. There are two kinds of insurance: *third* party and *(fully) comprehensive*.) / green card
7. A = saloon (called a *sedan* in AmE) / B = pick-up truck / C = motorcycle (also called a *motorbike*) / D = hatchback / E = city car / F = estate (called a *station wagon* in AmE) / G = MPV (*multi-purpose vehicle*, also called a *people carrier*, and known as a *minivan* in AmE) / H = scooter / I = sports car (a sports car with an open top is often called a *roadster*)

ANSWERS *(cont.)*

/ J = 4x4 (pronounced *four by four*. Called an SUV - *sport utility vehicle* - in AmE) / K = convertible (also called a *cabriolet* or *soft top*) / L = coach (a coach is also a passenger wagon on a train, for example, a *sleeping coach*)
8. A = classes (the main classes are *A, B, C, D, E* and *F*. Cars classed DW, EW and GW are small, medium and large *estate* cars. Cars classed 5M and 7M are *MPV's*. Cars classed BA, CA, DA, etc, are *automatic* rather than *manual*) / B = contract / C = paperwork / D = terms / E = conditions / F = CDW (collision damage waiver) / G = LDW (loss damage waiver) / H = personal / I = unlimited / J = drop-off / K = refuelling

Other words and expressions which you might find useful include:
airport access fee (for car hire companies) / congestion / city centre congestion fee (money that drivers must pay to enter the centre of some cities in their own vehicles) / pollution / rush hour / traffic-free zone (also called pedestrian zone) / Park and Ride (large car parks found outside many British cities to ease traffic congestion) / one-way street / no-through road / drink-driving / speeding

> ❋ Imagine that a foreign tourist visiting your country wants to hire a car for a few days and drive around the country. What advice would you give him / her (for example, rules of the road, tips for safe driving, etc)?

On the water (pages 40 + 41)

Exercise 1:
1. lifeboat   2. motor boat (also called a *speedboat*)   3. dinghy   4. hydrofoil   5. jet foil   6. yacht   7. ship
8. hovercraft   9. canoe   10. cabin cruiser   11. ferry   12. (ocean) liner   13. gondola   14. bumboat
15. narrow boat (also called a *long boat*)

Exercise 2:
1. False: it is called a *bareboat* charter (When a crew is provided, it is called a *crewed* charter. When crew, fuel, food and other provisions are included, this is a *provisioned* charter)   2. False: it must have a certificate of *seaworthiness*
3. False: it is measured in *knots*   4. False: the bow is the front and the stern (also called the *aft*) is the back   5. True
6. False: it is called the *deadweight* tonnage   7. False: the floors are called decks, the staircases are called companionways, and the captain stands on the bridge   8. True

Note that several words used for ships are also used for aircraft (for example, *port, starboard, fore, aft, knots*, etc)

Exercise 3:
1. marina / berths (berth is also a verb: *to berth*)   2. cabin / berths (= beds) / outside cabin / portholes   3. roll-on-roll-off (*ro-ro* for short)   4. Chamber / Federation / Maritime   5. embark / disembark   6. seasickness (the adjective is *seasick*)
7. crossings   8. convenience

Positive or negative? (page 42)

My hotel room was:
☺: airy   bright   charming   clean   comfortable   comfy (a colloquial short form of *comfortable*)   cosy   homely   huge   luxurious   quiet   roomy   spacious   spotless   sumptuous   well-kept   well-maintained
☹: basic (this word is *not* always negative: cheaper hotels and hostels often advertise their rooms as being basic, but this does not necessarily mean that the room is uncomfortable, small, etc)   boiling   claustrophobic   cramped   damp   dark   dingy   dirty   disgusting   draughty   filthy   freezing   horrible   icy   noisy   pokey   pretentious   scruffy   seedy   smelly   spartan (= *very* basic)   squalid   tiny   uncomfortable

The hotel food was:
☺: delicious   different (although this word could also be negative)   done to a turn (= perfectly cooked)   excellent   filling   healthy   lovely   mouth-watering   perfect   scrumptious (an informal word)   succulent (usually used to describe a piece of meat or fish)   sumptuous (usually used to describe a large meal with lots of different things to eat)   tasty   wonderful   yummy (an informal word, often used by children)
☹: awful   bland   boring   disgusting   fatty   greasy   horrible   inedible   indifferent   nondescript   oily   overcooked   overpriced (= too expensive)   revolting   repetitive   rubbery   tasteless   unappetising   undercooked   uneatable   unhealthy   vile   yucky (an informal word, often used by children)

The hotel staff were:
☺: affable   amiable   approachable   attentive   considerate   courteous   discreet   efficient   genial   helpful   kind   knowledgeable   lovely   pleasant   polite   smart (this word refers to their physical appearance: clothes, hair, etc)   warm   welcoming   well-mannered
☹: aggressive   discourteous   impolite   inattentive   indifferent   inefficient   insolent   lazy   off-hand   officious   rude   scruffy (this word refers to their physical appearance: clothes, hair, etc)   slack   surly   unapproachable   unhelpful   unpleasant

The tour we went on was:
☺: amazing   educational   fascinating   interesting   intriguing   riveting   stimulating
☹: boring   dull   mind-numbing   monotonous   soul-destroying   stultifying   tedious

The beach was:
☺: beautiful   lovely   picturesque   stunning
☹: crowded   dirty   heaving (= very crowded)   overcrowded   polluted   rocky   stony (*rocky* and *stony* are usually, but not always, negative when used to describe beaches)   windswept

Note that many of the adjectives in this exercise can be used to describe more than one thing. For example, a hotel room can be well-maintained, and so can a beach.

> ❋ Think of a holiday or a business trip you have been on recently. Describe your hotel room, the food you ate and the staff in the hotel. Did you go on any trips or excursions? What were they like? Try to describe other aspects of the trip (for example, your flight, the people you met, the places you visited, etc)

Prepositions (page 43)

1. from / to / at / on / during (or *in*) / at / on   2. by / from / to / on   3. at / at / from / through / in   4. into / in / for / in (or *at*)   5. on / by (or *at*) / outside (or *at*) / into (or *inside* or *around*) / for (or *on*)   6. at (or *in*) / by (or *near*) / from (or *to*) / to   7. with / with / of   8. to / with / for / since   9. with / for / to   10. to / in / in / at / with   11. for / to / for   12. for / in / of / to   13. as / like / like / like   14. on / for / in   15. from / on / of / in   16. over (or *around*) / on / to / in

Restaurants and bars (pages 44 + 45)

Wok and Roll = Chinese takeaway   Curry in a Hurry = Indian restaurant   Wetback's = Tex-Mex restaurant   Frank's Plaice = fish and chip shop (usually these are takeaway outlets, but some provide seating for their customers)   The Big Munch = fast food restaurant (also called a fast food outlet)   Souperman = diner   Bar Celona = tapas bar   Alhambra = bodega   Wasabi-Go! = sushi bar   Tastes = food court (also called a *hawker centre* in some countries, e.g., Singapore)   The Red Lion = pub   Mamma Mia's = pizzeria   Pasta Master = trattoria   Aux Trois Cloches = bistro   Le Poisson d'Or = relais (it could also be a *brasserie*)   Silverthorne's = carvery   Rosie Lee's = tea room   Jimmy's = snack bar (also called a *café* or *cafeteria*. Cafés which serve traditional British foods like English breakfasts, sausages and mashed potato, etc, are known colloquially as *greasy spoons*)   The George and Dragon = gastropub   Choo choo's = buffet

Other words which you might find useful include:
canteen   coffee shop   deli(catessen)   drive-through (often a feature of fast food restaurants)   family restaurant   sandwich bar   steakhouse   wine bar

> ❋ Recommend some restaurants and bars in your town / city to a visitor. What sort of restaurants are they? What do they serve? Are there any dishes that you would particularly recommend? Are there any places that the visitor should avoid? Why?

Services, amenities and attractions (page 46)

1. ATM (*automated teller machine*. We also say *cash machine* or use the trade name *Cashpoint*)   2. bus stop   3. botanic garden   4. port   5. internet café   6. guest house   7. Mosque   8. art gallery   9. police station   10. market   11. surgery   12. optician

The words and expressions in the box are:
Cinema (*theater* or *movie theater* in AmE)   art gallery   park   library   casino   airport   shopping centre (*mall* in AmE)   market   amusement park (also called a *theme park*)   stadium   youth hostel   nightclub   police station   bus stop   station   health club   ATM   restaurant   port   castle   bank   guest house (also called a *bed and breakfast* in Britain)   zoo   pub   museum   town hall   mosque   temple   surgery (= the place where a doctor works)   theatre   sports centre   taxi rank   post office   bar   chemist (also called a *pharmacy*, and a *drugstore* in AmE)   travel agency   phone box (also called a *public phone* or *pay phone*)   internet café   optician   botanic garden   ice rink (also called a *skating rink*)   dentist   hospital   beach

> ❋ What services and amenities are there in your town? What attractions are there for tourists to visit? Write a brief guide aimed at people visiting your town for the first time.
> Can you add any other services, amenities and attractions to the list in the box?

Travel equipment (page 47)

1. suitcase (the general word for something we use to carry things in when travelling is *luggage* or *baggage*. Other luggage / baggage types include: *rucksack* or *backpack*; *holdall* (see number 4); *shoulder bag*; *suit carrier*; *tote bag*; *trunk*; *pilot case*; *briefcase*. People use *bum bags* or *money belts* to carry money and other small valuables.)   2. torch (called a *flashlight* in AmE)   3. penknife (also called a *pocket knife*. If the knife features other accessories, such as

scissors, a screwdriver, a corkscrew, etc, we say *Swiss Army knife* (this is a registered trade name))   4. holdall   5. ticket
6. first aid   7. insurance   8. visa (types of visa include: *entry visa*; *multiple-entry visa*; *tourist visa*; *transit visa*)   9. work
permit   10. passport

The word in the shaded vertical strip is *toiletries*.

> ✸ Imagine that you are going to another country for two weeks, either on business or for a holiday. Make a list of
> 20 items you would take with you (not including clothes). These can be a combination of *necessities* (e.g.,
> passport) and *luxuries* (e.g., MP3 player). When you have made your list, try to reduce it to 10 items.

Travel health and safety (page 48)

1. first aid kit / fire blankets   2. altitude sickness (also called *mountain sickness*)   3. fire alarm   4. deep vein thrombosis
(also informally called *economy class syndrome*. It can affect anyone who has to sit in a small or confined space for a
long period of time)   5. safety announcement / safety card / emergency exit   6. motion sickness (also called *travel
sickness*) / air sickness   7. fire doors (also called *emergency exits*. Buildings may also have *fire escapes* that people can
use to get out of the building in case of a fire)   8. smoke detectors / carbon monoxide detectors   9. food poisoning
10. assembly point (on a ship this is called the *muster point*)   11. fire extinguishers   12. immunization (also a verb: *to
immunize*)   13. health declaration form / contagious (a disease that can be passed from person to person is also called a
communicable or *infectious* disease)   14. notifiable   15. upset stomach / hygiene

Some illnesses and diseases often associated with travel include:
cholera / dengue (fever) / diphtheria / hepatitis (types A, B and C) / Japanese encephalitis / malaria / rabies / tetanus / tick-
borne encephalitis / typhoid / yellow fever
Travellers arriving in a country who are suspected of carrying some contagious diseases may be placed *in quarantine*
(where they are kept away from other people to avoid *spreading* the disease). In many countries, all animals entering the
country are placed in quarantine. (*Quarantine* can also be a verb, usually passive: '*All animals are quarantined for a
minimum of six weeks*')

> ✸ Write an article for a travel magazine outlining the different things that travellers should do to remain fit and
> healthy, and avoid illnesses, while travelling.

Two-word expressions 1 (page 49)

Exercise 1:
accredited agent   boarding pass (also called *boarding card*)   cabin crew   departure tax   entrance charge   food
poisoning   general manager   handling charge   identity document (usually abbreviated to *ID*)   jet lag   key card
landing card   motion sickness   no-show   occupancy rate (also called *room occupancy*)   package holiday (a package
holiday that also includes food and drink in the price is often known as an *all-inclusive (AI)* holiday)   quality control
room number   service charge   terminal building   unaccompanied baggage   (opposite = *accompanied baggage*)
valet service   waiter service   youth hostel

Exercise 2:
1. cabin crew   2. jet lag   3. occupancy rate   4. package holiday   5. entrance charge   6. food poisoning
7. boarding pass   8. service charge (some restaurants also add a *cover charge*, and will also add *tax* is this is not
included on the menu price)   9. valet service   10. handling charge (also called *commission*)

Two-word expressions 2 (page 50)

1. Warsaw Convention   2. nature reserve   3. English breakfast   4. transit passenger   5. round trip   6. poste restante
7. excess fare   8.Eighth freedom   9. Mardi Gras   10. sightseeing tour (a tour to another place is also called an
excursion or a *day trip*)   11. reception room   12. Middle East   13. terminal building   14. ground handling   15. Gulf
States   16. sleeper seat

Types of holiday (pages 51 + 52)

Note that the types of holiday mentioned in this exercise are very specific. Many holidays would include elements of
several of these holiday types (e.g., people on a beach holiday might also do some sightseeing, and might be staying on
an all-inclusive basis).

1. self-catering holiday (this could apply to *any* holiday where the price of meals is not included in the holiday. Usually
abbreviated to SC in travel brochures. SC accommodation usually has cooking facilities so that guests can prepare their
own meals*)   2. adventure holiday (sometimes called *activity holidays*, especially if the activities offered are not
considered 'dangerous', e.g., canoeing, cycling, horse-riding, etc)   3. beach holiday   4. camping holiday   5. cruise
6. package holiday (people who go on package holidays are often referred to as *package tourists*. Those who prefer to
make their own travel plans are known as *independent tourists* or *travellers*)   7. skiing holiday   8. safari   9. hiking

holiday   10. all-inclusive holiday (often abbreviated to *AI* in travel brochures)   11. sightseeing holiday   12. sailing holiday (also called a *water-sports holiday*, especially if it includes other water-based activities such as *water skiing*, *windsurfing*, *diving*, *surfing*, etc)   13. environmental holiday (also called a *green* holiday)   14. tour   15. diving holiday (*PADI = Professional Association of Diving Instructors*)   16. working holiday   17. special interest holiday

* Holidays described as *half-board* (HB) include breakfast and dinner in the price of the holiday. Those described as *full-board* (FB) include lunch as well, and might also include snacks and afternoon tea. *Bed and Breakfast* accommodation (*B and B*, or *BB*) includes breakfast only.

Other holiday types include: backpacking holiday (A *backpack* is also called a *rucksack*. The verb is *to go backpacking*) caravanning holidays   fly-drive holidays   fly-cruise holidays   fly-rail holidays   weekend breaks   mini-breaks

> ✽ Choose some of the holiday types from this activity, and write your own advertisements or holiday brochure extracts. Try to make them sound as interesting and / or exciting as possible. Alternatively, design the 'ultimate' holiday package - one that includes lots of different activities - and write an advertisement for it.

Types of tourism (page 53)

1. responsible tourism (also called *green*, *soft* or *appropriate* tourism: the opposite of *hard* or *mass* tourism: see number 8)*   2. outbound tourism   3. roots tourism (also called *ethnic* tourism)   4. heritage tourism (similar to *cultural* tourism) 5. health tourism   6. agricultural tourism (also called *farm* tourism, or *agritourism*)   7. business tourism   8. hard tourism (also called *mass tourism*. Considered a slightly derogatory term, especially as it has a negative impact on the host country)   9. inbound tourism   10. religious tourism   11. incentive tourism

The word in the shaded vertical strip is *sustainable*. Sustainable tourism (also called *development tourism*) does not deplete natural resources or damage the environment, and does not have a negative cultural impact on the host community. In some cases it will even provide long-term benefits to the host community.

* Tourism which is believed to have a beneficial effect on the natural environment is often called *ecotourism*.

What has gone wrong? (pages 54 + 55)

1. undercooked   2. overcharged   3. delayed   4. lost (or stolen)   5. mugged   6. double-booked 7. misinformed   8. diverted   9. short-changed   10. poisoned (the noun is *food poisoning*)   11. stolen 12. burnt (we can also say *sunburnt*. The noun is *sunburn*)   13. robbed (note: a person, a room or a building is *robbed*, and belongings - for example, money, mobile phone, camera, etc. - are *stolen*)   14. damaged (*not* broken) 15. bumped (passengers are usually bumped when an airline deliberately or accidentally *overbooks* a flight. A passenger who checks in for the flight after other passengers have done so risks being bumped)

Note that when we describe an action but do not want or need to say who did it, we use the *passive voice* (e.g., He <u>has been mugged</u>, She <u>has been overcharged</u>). All of the gapped sentences in this exercise use the passive voice.

> ✽ Imagine you have recently been on a trip where a lot of things went wrong for you. Write a brief description of the trip and what went wrong, using some of the vocabulary from this exercise.
> For example: *First of all my flight was delayed by eight hours, then my luggage was lost…..*

What is their job 1? (pages 56 + 57)

1. cabin crew member on an aircraft (the words *air hostess* and *stewardess* are occasionally used for female cabin crew staff, but are usually considered old-fashioned and slightly sexist)   2. tour guide   3. waiter (or possibly chef)   4. pilot 5. check-in assistant at an airport (also called *ground crew staff*)   6. travel agent (the name of the shop they work in is called a travel *agency*. Note that a *travel agency* sells holidays which are provided by *travel operators* or *tour operators*) 7. holiday / travel representative (often abbreviated to *rep*)   8. barman (or *bar person*, to avoid sexism. *Bar staff* is a more general expression. Bar staff in *cocktail lounges* like to call themselves *mixologists*)   9. taxi driver   10. musician (e.g. pianist) in a bar or restaurant   11. police officer (or tourist police)   12. animator (sometimes called *entertainments director*)   13. customs officer

> ✽ If you are already working in the travel industry, describe the job you have now and outline your main duties. Alternatively, choose your 'ideal' travel job and write a description of the duties that it would involve.

What is their job 2? (pages 58 + 59)

1. manager   2. commissionaire (also called a *doorman*)   3. porter (also called a *bell hop* in AmE)   4. valet

ANSWERS *(cont.)*

5. concierge (often called a *head porter* in BrE, or *bell captain* in AmE)   6. receptionist   7. cashier   8. travel agent
9. chambermaid (also called *room maid* or just *maid*. Maids usually also work as *cleaners* in the rooms)   10. personal
assistant (abbreviated to *PA*)   11. meetings and conventions planner   12. comptroller (also called a *controller*, or
sometimes an *accountant* in larger hotels)   13. Maitre d'hôtel (usually abbreviated to *Maitre d'*. Also often called a *head
waiter*)   14. waitress   15. waiter   16. sommelier (also called a *wine waiter* or *chef de vin*)   17. greeter
18. sous-chef*   19. head chef (also called a *chef de cuisine* or *executive chef*)   20. plongeur

People in a hotel who deal directly with guests or customers are known as *front-of-house* staff. Those who do not deal
directly with guests are called *back-of-house* staff.

*A *sous-chef* (French for *under-chef*) assists the head chef in a restaurant kitchen. A large restaurant kitchen may also
have several sous-chefs, and also chefs in charge of a particular section: these are called *chefs de parties*. A chef de parti
may have assistants to help them: these are called *commis chefs*.

Other expressions which use the French word *chef* include:
chef entremétier (vegetable chef)   chef garde-manger (larder chef)   chef pâtissier (pastry chef)   chef poissonnier (fish
chef)   chef potager (soup chef)   chef saucier (sauce chef)   chef tournant (a chef who is available to work in any
section of the kitchen)

Where are they 1? (pages 60 + 61)

1. In a hotel   2. In a pub or bar (sometimes in a restaurant)   3. On a cruise ship   4. At the airport   5. In a restaurant
6. On a safari   7. On an aircraft   8. In a theatre   9. On an aircraft   10. In a taxi   11. On a bus   12. In a pub or bar*
13. In a restaurant   14. In an Internet café   15. On a sightseeing tour   16. At a ferry terminal   17. In a museum
18. On the beach   19. In a restaurant   20. At the airport

* Pub = *public house*. In a British pub, customers go to the bar to order and collect their drinks before taking them to a
table. Pubs do not usually have waiters and waitresses to serve drinks, but may use them to serve food.

Where are they 2? (pages 62 + 63)

1. On a cruise ship   2. At the airport   3. In a hotel   4. In a hotel   5. In an Internet café   6. On the beach
7. In a hotel   8. In a pub or bar* (ID = identification) 9. On an aircraft   10. In a hotel   11. In a pub or bar
12. On an aircraft   13. In a restaurant   14. On a sightseeing tour   15. At a ferry terminal   16. In a taxi
17. In a museum   18. In a theatre   19. In a hotel

* In the United Kingdom, the minimum legal age for buying alcohol in a bar or shop is 18.

❊ Choose one of the locations from the two exercises above, and write an extended dialogue between two people
(for example, between a customer in a restaurant and a waiter, or between an airline passenger and a check-in
assistant at the airport). Try to use some of the key vocabulary from the exercises.
